THEIR LAST WORDS

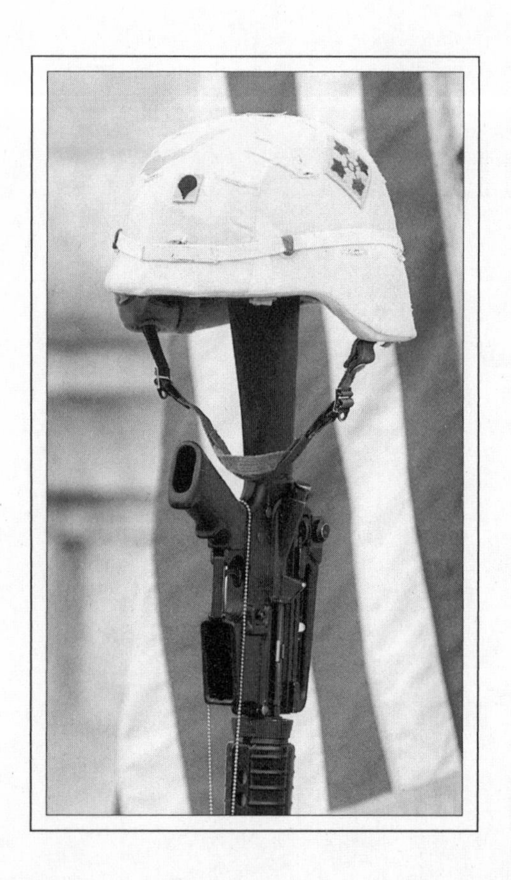

Berkley Caliber Books, New York

THEIR LAST WORDS

A TRIBUTE TO SOLDIERS WHO
LOST THEIR LIVES IN IRAQ

GEORGE G. SHELDON

THE BERKLEY PUBLISHING GROUP
Published by the Penguin Group
Penguin Group (USA) Inc.
375 Hudson Street, New York, New York 10014, USA
Penguin Group (Canada), 10 Alcorn Avenue, Toronto, Ontario M4V 3B2, Canada
(a division of Pearson Penguin Canada Inc.)
Penguin Books Ltd., 80 Strand, London WC2R 0RL, England
Penguin Group Ireland, 25 St. Stephen's Green, Dublin 2, Ireland (a division of Penguin Books Ltd.)
Penguin Group (Australia), 250 Camberwell Road, Camberwell, Victoria 3124, Australia
(a division of Pearson Australia Group Pty. Ltd.)
Penguin Books India Pvt. Ltd., 11 Community Centre, Panchsheel Park, New Delhi—110 017, India
Penguin Group (NZ), Cnr. Airborne and Rosedale Roads, Albany, Auckland 1310, New Zealand
(a division of Pearson New Zealand Ltd.)
Penguin Books (South Africa) (Pty.) Ltd., 24 Sturdee Avenue, Rosebank, Johannesburg 2196, South Africa

Penguin Books Ltd., Registered Offices: 80 Strand, London WC2R 0RL, England

This book is an original publication of The Berkley Publishing Group.

Cover design by Joni Friedman
Text design by Tiffany Estreicher

ISBN: 0-425-20385-9

PRINTING HISTORY
Berkley trade paperback edition: January 2005

This book has been catalogued by the Library of Congress

PRINTED IN THE UNITED STATES OF AMERICA

10 9 8 7 6 5 4 3 2 1

This one is especially for
Dallas William Sheldon.
He is another exceptionally fine grandson.

This one is especially for
Dallas William Sheldon.
He is another exceptionally fine grandson.

ACKNOWLEDGMENTS

Writing a book is never a one-man effort. The author might be the one who taps the words out on his computer or word processor, but there are many others who help make a book project possible. The book you hold in your hands is no exception. I want to acknowledge a long list of people for their contributions.

I certainly want to thank Mr. Jack Laukhuff of Lancaster, Pennsylvania, for his assistance and for providing me with background information and independent thought.

Special thanks go to my dear friend and fellow American Society of Journalists and Authors member Sondra Forsyth for her assistance. She provided me with special information that made this a better book.

All of the families, relatives, and friends of the fallen American soldiers depicted in this book are particularly appreciated for their help, kindness, and willingness to participate. I'm sure my questions were bothersome and painful at times; but again and again, they graciously allowed me to interrupt their lives. I want to especially thank Melissa Givens, Christine Dooley, Laurie Oaks, Paula Zasadny, Michelle Sorrel, Gregg Garvey, Camille and Jeffrey Hornbeck, Iratean Smith, Dawn Golby, Ronald Golby, Sonya Golby, Nadia McCaffrey, Gloria Caldas, Kathy Martin, Terry Cooper, Seth Martin, Patricia Roberts, Bridgette Van Dusen, and Kevin Addison.

Others that have helped me along the way include Donna Winter of Commerce, Wisconsin; John Washburn of Lyons, New York; Stefan Steudtel of Copperas Cove, Texas; and Deb Ellis of Littleton, Colorado. I also want to thank everyone else from the armed forces that assisted me.

I would like to especially thank Sergio Cardenas for providing me with perspective and insight, and for allowing me to use some of his words in this book.

Very special thanks go, as always, to Charles W. Byrd, my friend, fellow author, and mentor. Charles passed away in October 2003, just as I was conceiving of the idea of this book. He was the one who believed in me a long time ago, and he never stopped encouraging me over years of struggle. He is gone now, but he will never be forgotten. I will always remember his encouragement, passion, and friendship. I do miss him and wish he could see this book.

I also want to acknowledge the unwavering support of Bob DiForio, my literary agent, who brought this book to market. I appreciate his deep belief in the project from the first moment I contacted him. Thank you, Bob.

Special thanks go to my editor, Denise Silvestro, who did a great job of making my words better. Katie Day, her assistant, also helped to make this a better book, providing hours of patience in gathering photos and releases. Thanks to the wonderful cover designer, and everyone else at Berkley that made *Their Last Words* the best book it could be.

And a very special thank-you to my wife Gloria, who believed in me when no one else did. She helped tweak my prose, proofread for errors, and assisted with the typing and editing. Thank you for your wonderful and ongoing support.

FOREWORD

Perhaps the question most often asked of an author is, "Why did you write your book?"

There's no simple answer.

Writing is a journey of intensive labor—one that poses many challenges. The mere willingness to enter a period of seclusion is just one of the many sacrifices an author has to make. There are long hours of solitary writing and rewriting, as well as reading, studying, and just plain thinking. Editing, first by the author and then by the editor, follows this process. Only through dedication, sweat, and compromise are the final revisions to a manuscript made.

I found working on this particular book, though, to be harder than anything I've ever done before. My work often came to an unexpected, screeching halt. When those moments came, I simply could not write any more. I was too overcome with emotion brought on by the stories of the individuals in this collection. At times, I would just sit there in my darkened room, overwhelmed by the sacrifices these men and women made for our country. Often I would cry.

Those surges of raw emotion would come unexpectedly: like the time I learned that one of our fallen liked eating M&Ms, or playing the guitar. It was those kinds of small, ordinary facts that touched me the most. It is those kinds of facts that will bring these extraordinary people to life off the pages of this book.

These are *their* stories. These are the tales of Americans who honored themselves and their nation through their service. They came from diverse backgrounds, representing every thread that makes up the fabric of our nation. But they all had one thing in common: they *wanted* to serve. There was no draft that authorized their conscription. There were no strong-arm enlistment tactics. Each of the men and women in this book looked inside of themselves and found a call to duty.

I regret that there is only enough space in this book to write down some of the stories I've heard. There are many more to tell, many more tales of men and women who paid the ultimate price for their nation. These brave soldiers did not choose to serve, seeking glory or fame, but rather to fulfill their duty. And we, the grateful Americans they leave behind, will do whatever we can to return those that perish to their proper resting place, laying them to rest under an American flag, honoring and praising them for their service and sacrifice.

But just as we honor their deaths, it is important that we remember that they had dreams, hopes, and plans like the rest of us. They too had parents, spouses, significant others, and, for many, children, waiting for them to return home. They also understood the price of freedom and were willing to give all that they had to offer for the rest of us. It is a debt that is far beyond our power to ever repay.

I hope that this book will, in some small way, pay a lasting tribute to the men and women who chose to serve our nation and lost their lives in Iraq. Their sacrifices will never be forgotten. Their last words home will forever stand as a testament to their bravery and their everlasting love.

Why did I write this book? That's why.

George G. Sheldon
Lancaster, PA
August 2004

The Bean and the Toad

I will always be there with you, Melissa. I will always want you, need you, and love you in my heart, mind, and soul. Do me a favor. After you tuck Toad and Bean in, give them hugs and kisses from me. Go outside, look at the stars, and count them. Don't forget to smile.

—PRIVATE, FIRST CLASS JESSE A. GIVENS

When Jesse Givens first met Melissa Benfield, they were both working at a Shopko in Joplin, Missouri. She was a cashier; he was a security guard. That was only the first of their many differences.

Melissa already had a little boy, Dakota, who was just over a year old. Jesse was childless. A bookworm, Jesse read everything he could get his hands on, especially books by Stephen King and Tom Clancy. Melissa, on the other hand, preferred to see things on the big screen.

"Can't you wait to watch the movie?" she would ask as he lost himself in the world of words.

Years later, after the couple had relocated to Colorado, Jesse would often take time to enjoy the outdoors. He would call Melissa's attention to the many wonders of nature, particularly the mountains by their apartment.

"Yeah, a bunch of rocks. Can we go to the mall now?" she would reply (but always with a smile on her face).

Right from the start of their relationship, Jesse talked about a future and a family with Melissa. But she was hesitant—she was still young and wanted her freedom. She wasn't sure she was ready to commit herself to someone new. She had already been through one failed marriage, after all.

But as it turned out, Dakota made the decision for her.

"I had dated other people since I had Dakota, but he didn't like any of them," Melissa said. "But when Jesse was here, Dakota went over and put his hand on Jesse's knee and said, 'You my danny.' That was his way of saying 'daddy.'

"So I kept him. I figured, 'If the kid likes him, I'll keep him.'"

Danny wasn't the only nickname coined that day. At the time, Dakota could only halfway pronounce his name. He would call himself "Toat." But his new father thought it sounded more like "Toad," and the name stuck.

Jesse and Dakota at home

GIVENS FAMILY COLLECTION

When the Twin Towers of the World Trade Center fell on September 11, 2001, Jesse (who had always been described as "bighearted" by his friends) felt deeply wounded by the scenes of death and destruction he saw on TV. After the Shopko where he and Melissa had worked closed, he had found jobs here and there as an ironworker, and he watched in horror as his fellow iron tradesmen aided in the futile rescue effort at the WTC site. Seeing them dig through the twisted steel girders, he felt a deep pang of guilt.

"I should be there," he said to himself as he watched the news. "I should be there."

It didn't take him long to do something about it. He traded his ironworker's hard hat for a combat helmet. In December of 2001, Jesse enlisted in the army. He was thirty-two years old.

"And after the towers fell, he wasn't going to take anybody telling him, no, he couldn't [enlist]," Melissa says. "So he just went and did it without anybody's permission. And then he came home and told me."

Jesse's basic training graduation photo

GIVENS FAMILY COLLECTION

Melissa admits to being angry with Jesse when he told her what he had done. But she understood that it was the answer to a need he felt deep in his heart.

They spent Christmas of 2001 together. Then, in the beginning of January 2002, he was off to basic training in Fort Knox, Kentucky. At the ripe old age of thirty-two, Jesse had some niggling doubts about whether or not he would be able to keep up with the younger recruits, and when he arrived at Fort Knox, his fellow soldiers quickly took to calling him Grandpa. But Jesse never complained about the army's exhausting physical training. He just made it through. When the going got rough, he would think about Melissa and Dakota, and the thought of them would carry him.

Two big events occurred in Jesse's life after he graduated from basic training. Melissa finally consented to marry him, and the two were wed on June 4, 2002. Then he got his official assignment from the army: they had granted his request and stationed him in Fort Carson, Colorado, a place that perfectly suited his love of the outdoors. Jesse, Melissa, and Dakota packed up and moved west.

Life wasn't easy for the Givens family in Colorado. A serious mistake by the army's paymasters left Jesse without pay for six months. He diligently reported for duty each day, but returned home with empty pockets. He and Melissa had to go so far as to take out loans to pay for rent and groceries.

The Givens family

GIVENS FAMILY COLLECTION

But the family found happiness in each other's company. Jesse read books, took Melissa to parks, and played video games with Dakota. Even though they had limited funds, they indulged Melissa's love of the mall by frequently going window-shopping.

Even when things were at their worst, Jesse always found a way to lighten the mood.

"It's one of the things I miss now," Melissa says. "He made me laugh."

For Christmas 2002, Melissa and Jesse decided to try to make their first turkey together.

"Neither of us were good cooks," she admits. "I'm still a microwave chef."

Nevertheless, they worked together in the kitchen, mixing the stuffing and putting it "up the bird's ass." Then it came time to put the turkey in the roasting bag. Jesse pushed the well-greased turkey a bit too hard; it burst through the other side of the bag and fell to the floor. Never one to waste precious resources, Jesse quickly scooped up the stuffing that had fallen out of the turkey and rammed it back in. Despite the chaos, no one could tell the difference after it was roasted.

"It was good," Melissa remembers.

Jesse got in the habit of leaving notes around the apartment for his wife to find. He would write, "I love you," on a scrap of paper and place it on a package of bread or on the bathroom mirror.

Meanwhile, the Danny and the Toad were developing their own rituals. Jesse loved to eat Oreo cookies. He hid them on the top shelf of the cabinet, where he thought Dakota couldn't find them. But Dakota was quick to learn from his father and soon started hiding the packages *under* the cabinet. In the Givens household, it seemed that there were never quite enough Oreos to go around.

As relations between the United States and Iraq grew more strained, the Givens family got some wonderful news: Melissa learned

The Danny and the Toad

GIVENS FAMILY COLLECTION

she was pregnant. At the first ultrasound, the two parents-to-be marveled at the flickering screen. They were struck by the tininess of the embryo. It was barely the size of a bean.

Just like that, a new nickname was born. Though Jesse and Melissa agreed that the baby would be named Carson when he or she was born, throughout her pregnancy they referred to it as the Bean.

Jesse's unit received deployment orders for Iraq on Valentine's Day, 2003. He told Dakota that he had to go take care of a bad man who hurt people. He explained to his stepson that he did not want other little boys to grow up without their daddies.

On April 12, 2003, thirty-four-year-old Jesse Givens and the other fifty-two hundred men in his regiment, the Third Armored Cavalry, departed for Iraq, leaving Melissa, Dakota, the Toad, and the Bean behind.

Soon after Jesse left, Melissa inexplicably found herself searching through their apartment. She didn't know exactly what she was looking for, but she knew she would recognize it when she saw it. Finally she spotted a notebook in a carton and opened it. The message on the first page read, "If you are reading this, I have been deployed."

"He was always putting things where he thought I would find them. He knew me pretty well," Melissa remembers.

Over in Iraq Jesse was just as lonely. Although he knew he was doing his duty, Jesse felt as uncomfortable as Melissa did with his new life. He missed his wife and his children, and he had to walk three miles to make a single phone call.

"This place sucks," he would say to his wife. But more often he would simply repeat, "I love you. I love you."

On May 1, 2003, Private Givens and his team were given the duty of extinguishing fires set by Iraqi insurgents about thirty miles west of Baghdad. Even though the sixty-five-ton Abrams M-1 main battle tank he was driving was huge, Jesse was cramped into a small, constricted seat.

Suddenly, the tank crashed through a large berm, a high mound of earth at the river's edge, and plunged into the Euphrates. Every member of the tank crew escaped through the top—everyone except Jesse Givens. The tank's turret blocked his path to the escape hatch. The crew worked frantically to rescue him, but they couldn't reach him in time. Trapped in the driver's seat, his lungs filled with dirty, rushing water.

Private, First Class Jesse A. Givens was in Iraq less than one month when he perished. On the same day that President Bush declared an end to major hostilities in Iraq on an aircraft carrier thousands of miles away, Jesse Givens drowned in the middle of the dusty Iraqi desert.

A few days later, the sweaty soldiers of Fort Carson's Heavy Company filed into a bruised building located on a former Iraqi air base.

Positioned in front of the assembly was a pair of empty desert combat boots and an inverted rifle with its bayonet driven into the sand. A helmet rested on the butt end of the weapon.

First Sergeant Richard Banta called his unit to attention and started roll call. After the first several names, Sergeant Banta cried out, "Givens."

There was no answer.

"PFC Jesse Givens!"

No answer again.

And a third time, "PFC Jesse Givens!"

There was no response.

Outside, a group of soldiers fired their rifles in a salute and an army bugler played taps. Inside, the soldiers who had served with Jesse cried. It was their special way of saying good-bye to one of their own.

Specialist Tjuan Burt, the tank crew's loader, remembers a conversation he had with Jesse the evening before he died. They talked through the night about their families and how much they missed them.

Jesse made a tender, and chillingly prophetic, request of his friend. If something were to happen to him, he wanted Tjuan to give a message to Melissa: "Tell her I love her," Jesse asked. "Tell her I love her."

Tjuan recalled how frequently Jesse wrote to his family, and how he was hoping to get a letter from them soon. After his death, Heavy Company had a mail call. Givens's letter from home was on top.

"I'll never forget him," Tjuan says.

Jesse Givens died just days before what would have been his and Melissa's first wedding anniversary. On the same day that he passed away, Melissa went out and bought him an American flag. He had said he wanted it for the inside of his tank, which the crew had nicknamed Home Sweet Home. Only a few hours after she returned home, she was notified that Jesse was dead.

A memorial service was held at the Soldiers' Memorial Chapel at Fort Carson, even though there hadn't yet been time to bring Jesse's body back from Iraq. His fellow soldiers from the base were among the crowd of 250 that packed the chapel for his service. A lone bagpiper played a sad, lonely melody as the congregation filed past the steps of the altar where the same touching memorial that had appeared on the base in Iraq was on display: a pair of combat boots, an M-16 assault rifle, military dog tags, and a helmet.

Jesse Givens was posthumously awarded a purple heart, Bronze Star and an Army Meritorious Service Medal.

At the service, there was another roll call, a twenty-one-gun salute, and taps. The simple, beautiful notes were too much for Melissa and for many of the soldiers in attendance. They bowed their heads and cried.

When the army chaplain told Dakota that God had asked his stepdaddy to come to live with him, little Dakota bawled.

"He went to pieces, yelling that he didn't want God to have him, that he wanted to have him home," Jesse's mother Connie says.

Somehow, an eight-month-pregnant Melissa found the strength she needed to carry on—strength enough for her, for Dakota, and for her unborn child. She held Jesse's memory close to her heart. And just as he had left her notes in life, Jesse found a way to stay with her, even in death. On the day of their wedding anniversary, Melissa received flowers and a card from her late husband. Before he died, Jesse had asked his mother to, in the worst-case scenario, send his wife a bouquet. He told her exactly what to put on the card. It said, "Count the Stars, Love, Jess."

Then it happened.

Jesse's personal effects finally arrived home.

It was just a few days after Melissa had returned home from delivering her new baby boy: Carson Allen Givens, born exactly twenty-eight days after his father died.

There was a piece of Dakota's blanket, an old comforter made for Jesse's own mother before she was born. Jesse had taken a piece of the tattered blanket and braided it together to make a bracelet.

There was also the paper heart Melissa had given him the last Christmas. Virtually penniless, Melissa had given her husband the token as a gift, promising him that he would always have her heart. He had laminated it, as well as a small daffodil that Dakota had given him. Melissa also found a Seabees patch worn by his grandpa in World War II, along with a crucifix that his mother had given him.

There was one thing, though, that at first Melissa didn't see. The Friday before he passed away, Jesse had called her and told her about a letter he had written her, telling her not to open it unless he died. For the past few months, she had been waiting for it.

She finally found the mud-stained letter in his brown wallet.

"There is no doubt in my mind or my heart how much the three of us meant to my husband," Melissa says. "His letter to us was one of the most wonderful things I have ever gotten in my life."

Holding it, she sat on the front porch and cried her heart out.

"I needed that letter, and when it came, it was the saddest but one of the most comforting days in my life. I knew his love, and that he would always be with us."

After Jesse's death, Melissa released the letter to the media, and it quickly spread across the Internet. President George W. Bush included a passage of Jesse's letter in his Memorial Day remarks during a ceremony at Arlington National Cemetery in May 2004.

Carson at his daddy's memorial

GIVENS FAMILY COLLECTION

More than a year has passed since Jesse's death, but a twenty-seven-year-old Melissa says she still has good days and bad days. The rest of Jesse's division has trickled back, and it's been difficult for her to see joyful signs proclaiming, "Welcome home!" around town—especially when the signs are on the doors of her friends.

She has often thought about moving away from Fort Carson, but realizes that "this is my life." She only ventures onto the base itself when she needs medical care for her children. And she works to see the world through Jesse's eyes.

"I never stopped and looked at those mountains before," she said. "Now I do. I look at them the way Jesse did. I look at the stars the way Jesse would. They are beautiful."

Melissa pauses and then adds that Jesse would say, "The world is not a bad place."

She remembers that he once told her that he was going to stay with her for 150 years.

"By God, I am going to make him stick to it."

Jesse was a man who knew how to pursue his dreams. He loved the military, his country, and the outdoors. Above all else, he loved his wife and his family. As his last letter home makes clear, they never once left his mind or his heart.

My family:
22-*Apr*-03
I never thought that I would be writing a letter like this. I really don't know where to start. I've been getting bad feelings, though, and, well, if you are reading this . . .

I am forever in debt to you, Dakota, and the Bean. I searched all my life for a dream and I found it in you. I would like to think that I made a positive difference in your lives. I will never be able to make up for the bad. I am so sorry. The happiest moments in my life all deal with my little family. I will always have with me the small moments we all shared. The moments when you quit taking life so serious and smiled. The sounds of a beautiful boy's laughter or the simple nudge of a baby unborn. You will never know how complete you have made me. Each one of you. You saved me from loneliness and taught me how to think beyond myself. You taught me how to live and to love. You opened my eyes to a world I never dreamed existed. I am proud of you. Stay on the path you chose. Never lose sight of what is important again, you and our babies.

Dakota, you are more son than I could ever ask for. I can only hope I was half the dad. I used to be your "danny," but no matter what, it makes me proud that you chose me. You taught me how to care until it hurts; you taught me how to smile again. You taught me that life isn't so serious and that sometimes you have to play. You have a big, beautiful heart. Through life you need to keep it open and follow it. Never be afraid to be yourself. I will always be there in our park when you dream so we can still play. I hope someday you will have a son like mine. Make him smile and shine just like you. I love you, Toad. I hope someday you will understand why I didn't come home. Please be proud of me. Please don't stop loving life. Take in every breath like it's your first. I love you, Toad. I will always be there with you. I'll be in the sun, shadows, dreams, and joys of your life.

Bean, I never got to see you but I know in my heart you are beautiful. I know you will be strong and bighearted like your mom and brother.

I will always have with me the feel of the soft nudges on your mom's belly, and the joy I felt when I found out you were on your way. I dream of you every night; I will always. Don't ever think that since I wasn't around that I didn't love you. You were conceived of love and I came to this terrible place for love. I love you as I do your mom and brother with all my heart and soul. Please understand that I had to be gone so that I could take care of my family. I love you, Bean.

I have never been so blessed as the day I met Melissa Dawn Benfield. You are my angel, soul mate, wife, lover, and best friend. I am so sorry. I did not want to have to write this letter. There is so much more I need to say, so much more I need to share. A lifetime's worth. I married you for a million lifetimes. That's how long I will be with you. Please keep my babies safe. Please find it in your heart to forgive me for leaving you alone. Take care of yourself, believe in yourself; you are a strong, bighearted woman. Teach our babies to live life to the fullest; tell yourself to do the same.

I will always be there with you, Melissa. I will always want you, need you, and love you in my heart, mind and soul. Do me a favor, after you tuck Toad and Bean in, give them hugs and kisses from me. Go outside, look at the stars, and count them. Don't forget to smile.

Love always,
Your husband
Jess

SHADOW WARRIOR

If y'all are reading this, then I am on my way to help do my part to ensure the future security of our great nation. I don't take this charge lightly, or with a cavalier attitude, rather with a resolute heart and a clear conscience. I am strongly convinced that what we are doing is just, and worthy of all that could be spent in the effort.

—MASTER SERGEANT KELLY HORNBECK

The army's Special Forces have always been the stuff of legends. They are the elite—the best of the best. From counterterrorism to unconventional warfare, Special Forces units are trusted to get the army's toughest jobs done.

When they are called, they are called silently. They slip away in the darkness of the night and attack with precision. They perform quick-strike missions, using the element of surprise to disable their enemies with lightning speed and power. They complete special reconnaissance missions, sneaking behind enemy lines to gather vital information about locations, equipment, and weapons. They are spies and soldiers, fact finders, and finely tuned military machines.

The public knows them as the Green Berets. But the public's knowledge of what they do ends there.

Kelly Hornbeck was born in Selma, Alabama on June 28, 1967, into a military family—his father, Jeff Hornbeck, was an air force pilot. For that reason, his early childhood was geographically fluid. Kelly traveled with his parents to different military posts all over the world.

His father made sure, though, that Kelly had a happy childhood. He took his son hiking and camping and got him actively involved with the Boy Scouts. He didn't know it at the time, but he was planting seeds of passion for the outdoors that would stay with Kelly for the rest of his life.

The Hornbecks moved back to the States in 1983 and started to put down permanent roots in Fort Worth, Texas. And the young Kelly started to come into his own. During his junior year of high school, he joined the football team. Though he wasn't as naturally gifted as the other boys, he persevered. He started to develop the impressively strong work ethic that would become his trademark.

Kelly graduated from Paschal High School in 1985. He attended Tarleton State University for one year (and played on the football team). Then, in 1987, he made the decision to drop out of school and join the army—a fact that his air force father never quite let him live down. He quickly moved up the ranks from infantry soldier to drill instructor.

"He had an uncanny sense of knowing what a person needed," his dad says. "Whether that was a kick in the butt, a curse, or a hand on the shoulder, Kelly could assess a person quickly, and he was rarely wrong."

In 1990, Kelly volunteered for duty in the Special Forces. He trained and became a proficient combat diver, a free-fall parachutist, and a jumpmaster. His new lifestyle, though dangerous, fully immersed him in the two things he loved most in life: hard work and nature. One incident during Kelly's winter training exercise is a perfect example.

Kelly and his fellow Special Forces recruits were each given a radio and sent deep into the woods. It was a survival exercise. Their commander told them not to use their radios unless they had a serious emergency.

For some reason, once he got in the woods, Kelly moved from his documented position to what he considered to be a better location. Then a surprise blizzard dumped a heavy blanket of snow on his mountain.

For two days, his army comrades frantically searched for him. They called him on the radio, but Kelly didn't answer. They started to fear the worst.

They finally found him in a snow cave he had built, singing loudly to keep himself company.

"Why didn't you use the radio?" his commander demanded.

"You told me not to use it unless there was an emergency," Kelly calmly replied.

The incident didn't strike his father as at all strange. "He was the

Kelly in Iraq

HORNBECK FAMILY COLLECTION

happiest when he was outside. He loved camping and being in the field."

Kelly spent some time in Colorado for training and assignments, and he fell in love with the state's mountains. He developed a passion for mountain climbing, snow skiing, and snowshoeing. Along with adventuring outdoors, he took on several hobbies. His love of shooting old guns (complete with flintlocks and black powder) grew, as did his metalworking skills: he welded, built, and repaired metal objects. He also started to enjoy woodworking.

Meanwhile, his career in the army's Special Forces was flourishing. He was a self-made leader who led, above all else, by example. His strong work ethic earned him the respect of his commanders. Senior field officers sought his opinions about several different operations.

Like any good Green Beret, Kelly was a perfectionist.

"He was very intolerant of people not knowing what they were expected to do," his father recalls.

If he had any problem, it was that he was too good at his job: he earned so many badges, ratings, and medals that there wasn't room on his uniform to wear them all.

Rock climbing

HORNBECK FAMILY COLLECTION

Kelly met Caroline McKissick in Pinehurst, North Carolina (when he was stationed at the nearby Fort Bragg). The two instantly clicked. Both were divorced, single parents with children. Kelly had two daughters, Jacqueline McCall and Tyler Hornbeck. Caroline had a daughter of her own, Anna Grace. And they both shared a deep love of the outdoors.

"I knew we were meant for each other because he loved cross-country skiing," Caroline later told a newspaper reporter from the *Fayetteville Observer*. "How many people love to cross-country ski?"

They complemented each other. If there was a sport, activity, or skill one of them didn't know, it was a guarantee that the other did.

Much to Kelly's delight, the army reassigned him to Fort Carson, Colorado, shortly after he met Caroline. She didn't hesitate to move with him. Colorado would be the perfect place to continue their relationship. Kelly taught Caroline how to rock climb, and together they scaled Colorado's mountains and Utah's ice cliffs. They loved exploring the new landscape together.

"We spent so much time together backpacking, hiking, rock climbing," Caroline says. "He was a great outdoorsman. He taught me so much about the outdoors."

Jacqueline "Jake" McCall and Tyler Hornbeck

PHOTO BY JEFF HORNBECK

But, his new love notwithstanding, Kelly was still first and foremost a Special Forces soldier. His job required him to lead a life shrouded with mystery. It wasn't unusual for him to suddenly disappear for a length of time. Whether the mission was real or simply a training exercise, no one outside his elite group of soldiers really knew, not even his parents back home in Fort Worth, Texas.

Caroline—by then, his fiancée—was in the dark too. During the two years they were together, Kelly would often slip away. Sometimes when he returned, he would be wearing a bushy mustache or a straggly beard. Other times he came home looking like a well-groomed schoolteacher. For Kelly, it was all part of the job.

His dad, who had served in Vietnam, understood. Wherever Kelly went, he had a purpose and a reason. Jeff just assumed that his son "was always where the pot was bubbling."

Thirty-six-year-old Kelly Hornbeck deployed to Iraq on a classified date and time as part of the Third Battalion, Tenth Special Forces

Caroline and Kelly

HORNBECK FAMILY COLLECTION

Group. His division of Green Berets was charged with organizing Kurdish fighters in northern Iraq to battle Saddam Hussein's army.

He wasn't able to correspond with his fiancée or family very often. When he did, it was via satellite telephone. Kelly's position gave him access to special equipment. The conversations he had with them were vague, containing few specific details. But he did his best to ensure them all that he was doing well.

There were only three things that Kelly specifically asked his loved ones to send him from home. The first was beef jerky. The second was DVDs. His unit had a couple of portable DVD players, and movies were in high demand. Last of all, he asked for soccer balls.

There was an Iraqi school near where he was stationed. The school didn't have any academic or athletic supplies. When he told his mother Camille (an English teacher at Daggett Montessori School), she spread the word around the community. A few weeks after Kelly made his request, they shipped eight boxes of school supplies and sixty soccer balls across the ocean.

On January 16, 2004, everything went terribly wrong. Only a bit of tragically bad luck could have wounded a soldier as diligently prepared and thorough as Kelly Hornbeck. But such was his fortune that day.

He was riding in a patrol truck south of the Iraqi city of Samarra, leading his unit south, when an IED (improvised explosive device) detonated. The homemade bomb sent shrapnel in every direction. Somehow, a sharp piece of metal pierced the protective headgear Kelly was wearing, critically injuring him.

He was airlifted to an army hospital in Baghdad.

Later that day, back in Texas, Jeff Hornbeck got two phone calls. The first one was from Kelly's command post, advising his family of the incident. Then there was a call from a doctor. Kelly's prognosis was terrible.

"My knees buckled," Jeff remembers.

The surgeon told him that Kelly only had what doctors call "primal function" of the brain. To stay alive, he would have to be "artificially maintained." In other words, Kelly was brain dead.

The family knew that Kelly would never want to live his life hooked up to a respirator. They chose to disconnect life support. Two days later, Kelly died at the hospital.

Jeff and Camille Hornbeck met the press on the front lawn of their Fort Worth home the following Wednesday. They politely answered reporters' questions and told everyone what Kelly's death meant to them.

"He was doing a job he was called to do," Camille Hornbeck said during the news conference. "We just want to celebrate Kelly's life as a hero and to let the world know he is a special young man."

"We feel it is important to support the guys still doing their job," Jeff Hornbeck said as he held a portrait of his son.

"It is a very difficult task to build a democracy," he added.

Kelly's family wanted to make sure to encourage the soldiers who still had work to do in the Middle East.

Caroline McKissick, Kelly's fiancée, sold the house in Colorado and moved back to Southern Pines. She needed time to heal. She threw herself into activities that brought her comfort, like riding her horses, tending to her dogs, and hiking.

Then she decided to do something in Kelly's memory.

"I'd had this bug to do the Appalachian Trail for a while, and this was sort of perfect timing. My slate was pretty open," she said.

So in early spring, with snow still covering the mountaintops, she started hiking the 2,174-mile trail.

She pointed out that, if it hadn't been for Kelly, she never would have thought of making the journey.

Her trek across the Appalachian Trail, which concluded in the fall of 2004, raised money for the Fisher House, an organization that houses families of injured servicemen at veterans hospitals around the country. Caroline raised over thirty thousand dollars in pledges in Kelly's memory.

Back in a Fort Worth classroom, Camille Hornbeck was spreading her late son's dreams to the next generation of Americans. She told her middle school English students that Kelly died to defend liberty and to rescue Iraqis.

"I tell them it's not something I wished would happen, but Kelly felt committed to defending our country," Camille says.

By telling her students about her son's service, sacrifice, and dedication, she hopes to keep a little bit of Kelly alive.

Kelly's talent and dedication to life as a soldier are perhaps best described in correspondences that his parents received in the months following his death. Even the recruits that Sergeant Hornbeck barked at and disciplined in basic training called, wrote, or visited, to simply say thanks—thanks for helping them "get life in order."

Kelly wrote an undated letter to his parents that they received in November 2001. Jeff and Camille don't know where he was when he penned the note—one that would be quoted by President George W. Bush during his remarks at the Memorial Day Commemoration service at Arlington National Cemetery on May 31, 2004.

Though he was a man who kept his religious beliefs private, Kelly spoke openly of his faith in the letter. He never discussed religion with his parents or his fiancée, but it's clear that he had a deep faith in

God. Perhaps that was fitting for a soldier, and a man, who kept so much of himself hidden from those he loved, all in the name of his country.

Master Sergeant Kelly Hornbeck
HORNBECK FAMILY COLLECTION

Dear Mom and Dad:
If ya'll are reading this, then I am on my way to help do my part to ensure the future security of our great nation. I don't take this charge lightly or with a cavalier attitude, rather with a resolute heart and a clear conscience. I am strongly convinced that what we are doing is just and worthy of all that could be spent in the effort. I am not afraid and neither should either of you be, for I trust in my God (Psalm 23) and my training, two powerful forces that cannot be fully measured.

My training is not only limited to that which has been bestowed on me by the mightiest military in the world but also by the greatest set of parents in the world. I am who I am because ya'll made me that way, and for that I thank you.

If anything untoward should befall me, please ensure that the qualities you raised me with get passed on to my children. I love you both very much and intend to see you soon!

Isaiah 6:8
Kelly

The Shy Guy

Mom, read this letter to as many people as you can, especially to my loving sister, Talisha. Let them know to appreciate where they're at, and that we're still here fighting to help Iraq and defending our great country.

—STAFF SERGEANT ORENTHIAL J. SMITH

Martin, South Carolina, is a typical small Southern town. Nestled a few miles north of the Savannah River, just inside the Georgia–South Carolina border, it isn't much more than a railroad crossing, two churches, and some occasional traffic from Route 125. It's one of those Southern communities that's sometimes hard to notice, even if you're driving through it.

Orenthial J. Smith lived in Martin with his mother, Iratean, and his younger sister, Talisha. He was as shy as his hometown was small.

"He was always a skinny kid," his mother says. "And he always wore glasses. It gave him a nerdy look."

But being shy didn't stop Orenthial—nicknamed O.J.—from being imaginative and inquisitive. Iratean remembers how, as a little boy, he dreamed of driving big trucks. Even though he had plenty of toy Tonkas lying around, he would cut up cereal boxes and turn them into trucks.

When he wasn't on the floor playing with his creations, O.J. was reading books.

"He was a bookworm," Iratean says.

"I remember when he was approximately five years old, the words that he would pronounce were unbelievable," O.J.'s aunt, Betty Thompson, recalls. Both Iratean and Betty would constantly remind the young boy about the importance of education.

O.J. in 1st grade

SMITH FAMILY COLLECTION

Early on, the message seemed to stick: during his elementary and middle school years, O.J. earned A's and B's. But as soon as he hit high school, he started to slack off.

"He was a pretty good student, but he did not try as hard. His A's and B's went to B's and C's," Iratean says.

His mother thinks peer pressure was behind it. She knows kids called him a nerd because of his appearance. Lanky, tall, with round gold-rimmed glasses on his face, he looked like the stereotypical geek featured in every teenage movie. To top it all off, his favorite subject in school was math.

When O.J.'s sixteenth birthday rolled around, his mother decided she'd had enough. She sent him to summer school. What's more, she told her son that he would be responsible for repaying the extra tuition money she was going to spend.

O.J. diligently attended his summer classes and got a job as a cook at the Sonic Drive-In in Barnwell, South Carolina. In just one summer, he started to get himself back on track.

When he returned to Allendale-Fairfax High School in the fall of 1996, O.J. joined the football team. He was a wide receiver and a kicker. He didn't come close to playing in every game, but he was content. His coach, Carlos Cave, recalls that he was happy just being

O.J. in 11th grade, on the football team
SMITH FAMILY COLLECTION

part of a team.

"He liked the camaraderie and the relationships he built with the guys he played with," Carlos would later tell a reporter.

Carlos continued reminiscing about what kind of player O.J. had been. "He tried extra hard. He always did whatever was asked of him."

By the time he was a junior, O.J. had made it back on the honor roll.

It was about halfway through his senior year of school that O.J. was struck by the idea of enlisting in the army. At first, his family was very taken aback. His aunt, Betty, pleaded with him.

"I said, 'Orenthial, you can attend almost any college that you want.' He said, 'I want to join the army.' We finally accepted it, knowing that he had made up his mind."

Thirteen days after O.J. Smith graduated from high school in June of 1999, he enlisted.

The shy, skinny six-foot, one-inch Martin native had a tough time in basic training. He especially disliked the "in your face" training he got from his boot camp drill instructors. But he survived. He went on to become what the army calls a petroleum supply specialist: he drove a fuel tanker truck.

Surprisingly, post-basic training army life seemed to agree with him. O.J. had planned to stay in for only two years. But when his commitment expired, he reenlisted for six more.

Once he got through basic training, he said he loved the army. When he was home on leave, he chose to wear his uniform to church. He wore his army-issued tee shirts and fatigues around the house or on errands.

O.J.'s high school graduation photo

SMITH FAMILY COLLECTION

During one of those visits home, he gave some important advice to his little sister.

"Study harder," he told her.

"He'd tell me that if I got a B, I should try for an A," Talisha remembers. He constantly pushed her to strive for academic excellence.

As proud as he was of his own service, O.J. talked Talisha out of joining the military. He was still, first and foremost, a brother. He wanted nothing more than for her to stay in school at USC (the University of South Carolina) and get her degree.

Slowly but surely, the army was bringing O.J. out of his shell. He was given a position as a truck driver with the army's 123rd Main Support Battalion, based in Dexheim, Germany. An ocean away from home, O.J. shed the last of his shyness. He impressed his superiors so much that they encouraged him to train for a promotion to sergeant.

Just as he had done in school, O.J. excelled when he applied himself. When he completed the training course, he took the sergeant's exam.

O.J. telephoned home while his aunt was visiting his mother. "I was at his mother's house when he called," Betty recalls. "He told me that he had completed the leadership course for sergeant and had graduated 9th out of 127. I will never forget the words he said to me."

She remembers O.J. saying, "Aunt Betty, thanks for everything, for not giving up on me. I could have never done it without people staying on me. I can't believe that I have accomplished so much in such a short time."

Bursting with pride, Iratean, who was working as a machine operator in a fan-belt factory in Williston, South Carolina, sent a notice to the local newspaper. Soon, the whole town knew that her son had graduated from the army's leadership development course with a grade point average of 94.56.

The once shy boy now carried himself with pride and purpose.

"His voice was full of joy, excitement, and happiness. He always walked as if he had many things to do, all in a hurry," his Aunt Betty says. His newfound confidence even prompted him to pursue a degree in computer technology at his post in Germany.

Orenthial J. Smith, March 2003

SMITH FAMILY COLLECTION

O.J. managed a trip home for the holidays in 2001. He still loved spending time in the gentle hills and pastures of the South. Back in his mother's house, he indulged in his other boyhood passion: Sony PlayStation. But all too soon for Iratean, the vacation ended. In January, he returned overseas.

O.J. made sure that he

spoke to his mother once a week on the telephone. He always checked on his sister's progress in school and prodded his mom to ensure that she kept up with her studies. Meanwhile, his mother sent him care packages that included Kool-Aid, Cheetos, and special chocolate pies that he loved to eat.

He grew close to the other soldiers stationed in Germany. A group regularly gathered to watch NASCAR races on Sundays. O.J.'s favorite driver was Dale Jarrett.

"Every time he won a race, Smith would see me the next morning at work and let me hear how his guy beat mine. From two blocks away, Smith would spot me and yell out, 'Dale Jarrett, baby!!!' I could never do anything but smile," one army buddy recalls.

"If I, or anyone for that matter, ever needed anything, we knew Smith would always be in his room," another friend would later write on a Web site bulletin board. "Because that's where he spent a lot of his time, preparing his uniform and boots for the next day. The constant soldier."

O.J. and his cousin, Roosevelt Jr., at a family reunion in 2000

SMITH FAMILY COLLECTION

O.J. had been in Germany for more than a year when he received deployment orders for Iraq.

"I'll be fine," he told his beloved sister on the telephone and tried to change the subject to sports.

On May 6, 2003, O.J. left Germany for Kuwait. Once he arrived in the Persian Gulf, his calls to home grew farther and farther between.

But even from his sporadic correspondences, it was clear how powerfully his experience in Iraq was affecting him. He told his mother about how many Iraqis he saw lining the road from Kuwait to Baghdad, "hoping we would throw them some food and water." Even though the army had warned its soldiers not to give any handouts as they drove along, O.J. often couldn't stop himself. He said to his mother, "I couldn't stand to see how poorly the Iraqis live."

He called home for the last time in mid-June. His mother would later say that there was something haunting about the call.

"Sometimes, I really wonder if he had a premonition," Iratean reflects. "When he was finished talking, he kept saying, 'I love you, Mom. I love you, Mom.' It was like he just didn't want to hang up."

On Sunday, June 22, 2003, O.J., who was serving with the army's First Armored Division, received word that he had been promoted to sergeant.

Only a few hours later, he was killed when his convoy was attacked in Baghdad.

Talisha was home alone when a uniformed soldier knocked at the front door. She called her mother who was at work, trying to earn some overtime pay. There was a soldier waiting, Talisha said, with a message for them.

"I knew right away what it was about," Iratean remembers.

When she arrived home, "I didn't give the guy a chance to talk. I just started screaming." She remembers thinking, "If I didn't let him talk, he couldn't tell me and it wouldn't be true."

But there was nothing she could do to change the awful reality.

Today, Iratean's most comforting thoughts come from O.J.'s last letter home. She often cradles it in her hands, caressing the paper with a mother's loving touch. She looks at her favorite passages and reads them aloud. She still finds herself moved by her twenty-one-year-old son's descriptions of the squalor and terror of life in Iraq, and his reflections on how much better the world is back in Allendale County, South Carolina.

Until the soldier showed up at her door with the mission of notifying her of her son's passing, Iratean Smith says she always believed O.J. would come back safely to Martin. In his letter, he promised, "We will return home."

But she knows he died doing something he truly wanted to do, in a uniform that he loved to wear. Both she and Talisha find solace in knowing that their only son and brother died fighting for his country.

Talisha says, "I will always remember him as a loving brother who was a fighter that never gave up. He stuck by me through thick and thin. He never gave up on me, and he always put other people first before himself."

His mother adds, "I would love to have him here for another fifty-some years. He was a gift from God. But I just say now that he had served his purpose on Earth, and now he's in heaven to help out as an angel."

7 Jun 03

Dear Mom:

How you doing? Great, I hope. I'm just writing you to let you know that I'm doing fine, but that the living conditions are worse. We often have sandstorms so powerful that air blows down the tents we sleep in, and sometimes we run out of food and ice we use to have a nice cool drink. When I was in Kuwait, I couldn't tell you much on the phone because the intelligence personnel were keeping a close watch over the phones and if you said anything that you're not supposed to say about the war such as dates and where you're at, also what you're doing, the phones would automatically cut off. When we drove from Kuwait to Baghdad, it took us thirty-two hours to get where we were supposed to be. By the time we crossed the Iraq-Kuwait border, Iraqis were lined up on the side of the road waiting for us to pass by, hoping that we would throw them food and water. We're not supposed to throw them food and water, but I had to because I couldn't stand to see how poor the Iraqis live. Man, the people in Iraq live so poor that most of them don't have shoes to walk in. I'm talking about from kids to the elderly. Their houses are made of dry-strong mud clay with no roofs and no floors. The floor in their homes is the ground itself. Their clothes are so worn out that they have holes in them, and most of them have only one set of clothes. The kids are so cute but they live so poor. When they're lined up on the side of the road, they give us hand signals asking us to give them some food, water, clothes, shoes, money, weapons to protect them from the rest of Saddam Hussein's regime. They mostly want rides to leave their homes to go to paradise. Also, the parents of the children will tell their kids to go into the middle of the streets of moving traffic to stop us so they can steal whatever we're carrying. Then you have the other Iraqis that are against us, firing their weapons at us when we drive by. We react by firing back. When they shoot at us, they shoot at everybody, including the other Iraqis that are poor and against Saddam Hussein. It's sad to say that my partner in the truck with me was shot in the shoulder, breaking his collarbone, and as for my truck, it's a total disaster. The truck caught on fire, the wheels blown out because of bullets, and bullet holes all over the truck. Thank God my partner is still alive today. He's doing fine, walking with a sling on his right arm, saying thank you to us for saving his life. When he got shot, I couldn't be-

lieve that my partner was injured. Thanks to the training that we received, I reacted quickly by firing my machine gun back to protect us, so that the rest of my comrades could render first aid to my partner. After we fought them off, I looked towards heaven and said, "thank you God for still keeping us alive," because for a minute, I thought I was going to lose my life. We encountered a lot of attacks against us going to Baghdad, but we made it through. There is still more to come. Even though the President said that most combat operations in Iraq are over, this war still continues. There are still soldiers, sailors, airmen, and marines dying here. The reason the media doesn't cover the war anymore is that they want to see a lot of action going on, instead of just having an attack here and another one a couple of days later. Let everyone know that there are Americans here with their lives on the line for our country. Some appreciate what we do and some don't. But I have a message for those that don't: You think it's easy to live in a different type of environment away from your loved ones? You think it's easy to live through sandstorms so bad that you can't breathe for all the sand and dust in the air? You think it's easy not to have three home-cooked meals a day and something cool to drink? You think it's easy to see human beings like yourself living in a state of poverty with bad homes, with little or no electricity, no shoes to walk in, barely any food to eat. No money or income, barely any vehicles to ride to stores (if they have any stores in their local community), bad clothes, no kind of protection, having to bargain with people that are not a part of your culture and country to help you live, no good medical care, and not the right type of government to help lead a country to a better world? You think it's easy to protect yourself from the enemy that's actually trying to kill you? You think it's alright to see your partner almost lose his or her life in your arms? Now picture that was you going through this. Mom, read this letter to as many people as you can, especially to my loving sister, Talisha. Let them know to appreciate where they're at and that we're still here fighting to help Iraq, and also defending our great country. I would like to take this opportunity to say thank you to each and every one of you for your prayers, support, signatures on the spiritual card, and most of all the love and respect you have for us. Just remember, without you supporting us, this wouldn't be possible. Even though you're not on the battlefield fighting the battle and going through the amount of stress we're facing, you're still a part of this war. Again, thank you for what you do, and I ask that you continue to support us in every way you can. From all of us on the front lines, thank you, we love you America, and we will return home.

Orenthial Smith
SPC (P) Smith, Orenthial
U.S. Army

P.S. Here's a present to you that a little Iraqi girl gave me when I issued food and water to her. I love you Mom, Talisha, and the rest of the family. Take care and I WILL BE HOME!

No Fear

I love and miss you guys sooooo much. I promise I'll be safe.

—PRIVATE, FIRST CLASS HOLLY J. MCGEOGH

Holly McGeogh had always been fearless.

By the time she reached the tender age of fourteen, she was already addicted to the thrill of extreme activities. One time, on a family vacation to Tennessee, she insisted on going bungee jumping. Her mother, Paula Zasadny, was apprehensive about it, and at first, she refused to sign the permission slip Holly needed. But Holly was as determined as she was daring, and she found a way to make her wish come true: she had her dad sign the form.

As the years passed, Holly's fearlessness—and her independence—grew along with her. Although in some ways, she was just a typical teenage girl who loved to shop at Banana Republic and Old Navy and whose favorite color was blue, many of the things she did set her apart. For one thing, she loved to go squirrel hunting with her stepfather, Michael Zasadny, the man she called Dad.

Holly wasn't a squeamish teenager. She skinned the squirrels that she shot, just as her dad taught her to do. She loved the adventurous trips her family took to their hunting cabin deep in the northern woods of Michigan, everything from the lack of indoor plumbing to long canoe trips down the river. As a teenager Holly might have learned to appreciate the art of shopping, but her daring spirit was still alive and well.

Almost too well, Paula might say. Back in Taylor, Michigan, Holly struggled to keep her grades up. She didn't like math or English and was satisfied to squeak by with D's.

"She could have done a whole lot better than she did," Paula says. "She didn't really apply herself."

Sometimes, if her grades were too poor, Holly's mom grounded her.

"It's not fair!" Holly pleaded.

"Welcome to growing up," her mom replied.

Then, during her freshman year at Truman High School, something happened: Holly suddenly took an interest in the army's JROTC (Junior Reserve Officer Training Corp) program. After weeks of talking incessantly about it, she decided to sign up. Once a week she wore her green uniform to school. Soon it became clear that the lessons she was learning as a cadet, including ethical values, good citizenship, leadership, and how to work as part of a team, perfectly complemented the lessons she was learning in the classroom. It wasn't long before her uniform was covered with the ribbons and medals that she had earned.

In some ways, it was surprising that this new regimented lifestyle suited Holly's adventurous personality.

"When she was in tenth grade she told me she wanted to join the army," Paula says. "I laughed and said, 'You can't even keep your room clean, and you want to join the army? If you want discipline, I'll show you discipline.'"

What's more, Holly had been born with one lazy eye. Although as a small child she wore a patch over her good eye in an effort to strengthen the muscles around her bad one, she had worn glasses almost all her life and was nearly legally blind on her right side. (Later, it would take Holly three separate physicals before army doctors cleared her.) If she was really going to pursue her dream of joining the military, it was clear that she was going to have to overcome several obstacles.

But of course, Holly persevered, pushing herself to excellence in the JROTC program. As it turned out, as her senior year drew to a close, the only thing keeping her from the armed services was the same voice of restraint that had been there all her life: her mother's. Because Holly was only seventeen, she needed her mother's permission to join the army's delayed enlistment program. And Paula's first answer was an unequivocal "no." But Holly wouldn't be denied.

"Mom, you always said, 'I don't care what you do as long as you like it and give it your all,'" Paula recalls her saying.

"She made me eat my words and realize that I was being selfish. So I signed the consent form," Paula said. And made Holly's dream a reality.

The soldier and her mom, Paula, at a graduation party

PHOTO BY MICHAEL ZASADNY

Holly at her high school graudation

PHOTO BY PAULA ZASADNY

Soon, the Michigan teen was off to Fort Jackson in South Carolina. With her typical boundless energy, Holly (who was only five foot, three inches) shone in the army's basic training program. In fact, she loved it! Later, after the basic training graduation ceremonies, Paula remembers one of Holly's drill sergeants telling her, "You got one helluva soldier there. She may be the only private to ever complete basic training thinking, 'It was fun.'"

On the firing range, Holly even overcame the challenge of using her left eye to fire her rifle. It took time and effort, but she qualified twice.

"She was so excited," Paula remembers. "She called me to say, 'Mom, I finally did it!'"

After graduation, Holly was off to Fort Hood, Texas, for AIT (advanced individual training). Holly's testing showed she was well suited to be a light-truck mechanic. Soon she found herself in a motor pool, maintaining the army's Humvees and other smaller vehicles. She graduated from AIT having been appointed a class leader.

On January 31, 2003, Holly was assigned to the Fourth Infantry Division, A Company, Fourth Forward Support Battalion at Fort Hood. It was her first permanent duty station. A week later, she received deployment orders for Iraq. She was incredibly excited about the opportunities—and the adventure—that the trip would offer.

Her unit left on April 3, 2003. After a twenty-four-hour plane ride followed by a twenty-two-hour convoy through Kuwait, Holly and her unit, Company A, Fourth Forward Support Battalion attached to the 4th Infantry Division (MECH), found themselves stationed outside one of Saddam Hussein's former palaces in Tikrit.

Holly sent her family a steady stream of letters, e-mails, and phone calls when her work schedule permitted. Those correspondences made it clear just how much Holly loved her job.

"She told me many times," Paula says. "In every picture she is smiling ear to ear, even in the one where she's hog-tied during an initiation in Iraq."

After four months, Holly finally had a chance to talk to her mom on the telephone. She mentioned that she hadn't been able to take a shower since she arrived.

Holly's basic training graduation photo

McGEOGH FAMILY COLLECTION

"How can you stand not showering?" her incredulous mother asked.

"It's no big deal, Mom. We all smell the same."

Paula says that at that moment she realized how many everyday things we take for granted.

Paula tried to make

Holly's life a little sweeter by sending her packages laden with her favorite goodies: bottles of ketchup and barbeque sauce to spice up the bland army food, Cherry Twizzlers, Sour Cream Pringles, Mountain Dew soda, and blue Tommy Hilfiger sleepwear. She even found a way to deliver Holly's favorite hot sauce from Taco Bell.

"I ate a lot of Taco Bell food to get those packets to send her," Paula remembers ruefully.

Holly loved getting the packages her mother sent. In one e-mail home, she told Paula that getting those boxes made her feel like it was Christmas. In the same e-mail, she gave her mother another piece of news that made her very happy: Holly told her she was planning on taking correspondence courses online. She was even thinking of having some textbooks sent to Iraq.

On August 11, 2003, Holly wrote to one of her friends who had just enlisted. Helena Westmoreland joined the army because of the influence Holly had on her in high school. The soldier offered Helena a three-page letter full of advice for a new recruit getting ready for basic training. It includes the following words.

Helena,

Hey Chicka, waz ↑? I just got your letter yesterday. I was so happy to hear you again. I miss you lots & lots.

I wish that I could have been there for you, before you left. We would have had a blast! I bet you were real nervous before you left. You probably understand. I remember crying myself to sleep quietly every night at reception. That place sucks the worse. I was also so scared. I missed everyone so very much. But believe it or not, I had so much fun doing everything. Of course I was scared shitless & you're going to learn things & do things you never thought possible before. They're going to break your body & mind down, & then build you back up. I want to tell you something & don't ever forget it. "Never *give up!" No matter what, you do it. Because if you don't get done the first time, you have to do it again &*

again. You'll make things harder for yourself. Stay motivated! *No matter how bad of a mood you're in. Always be motivated! I'm telling you these things because I learned them myself & have seen what happens to other people. I want you to be the best you can be. Remember, if* I *can do it,* you *can do it . . .*

Anyways chick, I gotta lay it down for the night. It's almost 1:00 a.m. in the morning. It's about 5:00 p.m. for you (well 1700 hrs.) I promise I will write real soon. Please, find some time to write me back & let me know how you are. All I need now is your address. Hopefully my mom has gotten it. I'll get it from her.

Anywho, see ya soon! So . . .
Love ya lots, Chick!
Keep your head up. Everything is going to be okay
Your best friend,
Holly

P.S.—I could never, ever forget you! Remember that! You are my Best Friend in the World!

On August 29, 2003, Holly celebrated her nineteenth birthday.

It wasn't easy for Paula and Michael to be so far away from their little girl, knowing she was in danger. In fact, after Paula first found out that Holly was going to Iraq, she started taking antidepressant medication. In October, Holly's parents had to suffer through a couple of particularly nerve-shattering days when the news broke that a female soldier in Holly's unit had been killed in action. On October 1, 2003, Holly's friend and roommate, Analaura Esparza-Gutierrez, a twenty-one-year-old private, first class from Houston, Texas, was killed in a convoy hit by an improvised explosive device and rocket-propelled grenades in Tikrit. But the news stories in Michigan only said the victim was a "female soldier." Two days later, after the story broke, Holly telephoned. It was a conversation that Paula would never forget.

"Oh, my God!" Paula cried out when she heard her daughter's voice on the phone. Holly was crying, but not because she was scared. She was mourning the loss of her friend. It was, according to Paula, the only time she heard her daughter cry while she was in Iraq.

"Thank God, you're okay!" her mother said gratefully.

"Damn it!" Holly exclaimed. "I am doing exactly what I want to do."

She had more to say to Paula. Composing herself, she spoke. "If I die tomorrow, you have to remember that I died for a purpose and a cause I truly believe in."

"And those words I will remember for the rest of my life," Paula now says.

Never once in e-mails, letters, or phone calls did Holly express a desire to come home. She had some tough days, when it seemed like nothing went right—when the trucks she was working on were filled with problems and glitches, when the temperature spiked over 130 degrees. But Private, First Class Holly McGeogh persevered.

Paula remembers one moment in November of 2003 that stands as a testament to Holly's ability to be positive about any situation. Her

Paula and her Willy

PHOTO BY MICHAEL ZASADNY

younger brother, Robbie, had tried to transfer Holly's stereo system into his room without asking permission (before getting caught red-handed by their father). He didn't feel too bad about it. His older sister had picked on him for years.

During a telephone conversation, Paula happened to mention her brother's indiscretion. Holly made a snap decision.

"Mom, I want you to take the money out of my account and buy Robbie a stereo for Christmas," she told her mother.

Her mother wasn't sure she had heard her right.

"Take $250 out of my account and buy it for him," Holly reiterated.

Paula thought Holly should be the one to give him the good news. Robbie was roused out of bed at 2:30 in the morning to speak on the phone to his sister. Paula could only hear one side of the conversation, but she could tell exactly what was passing between the two.

"No way!" Robbie said in excitement. "Okay I love you too."

It was the first time in a long while that Paula had heard the siblings say that they loved each other.

Holly and her brother, Rob, as children

PHOTO BY PAULA ZASADNY

As the holidays approached, Holly was able to write a few more letters and e-mails than usual. In one poignant e-mail, she told her mom that she and her fellow soldiers had started just saying, "Christmas," to each other because December in Iraq wasn't very merry. She managed to send a Christmas card to each member of her family. She signed the one to her mother "Willy," a nickname Paula gave her when she was just a baby.

Mom,
Hey, Momma, just want to say that I hope you have a good Christmas & a Happy New Year. I know it won't be the same. It's gonna be different for me, my first Christmas ever by myself. I gotta be strong & so do you. So please put on the Santa hat & have some fun. If you decide to get drunk, drink some Captain Morgan's Spiced Rum & some Dr. Pepper for me.—k—!

Remember when I get back we're gonna go shopping & get pampered. A whole week together. And you're not gonna need those pills anymore. So we can throw them out.—k—

But anyways, I love you with all my heart & I couldn't ask for a better mom cuz I got the best one in the world already!

Have a Merry Christmas & a Happy New Year!
Love with all my heart,
Willy
2003

She sent a separate card to her father:

Dad,
Hi, Daddy. How's it going? I'm doing good. I want you to know that I couldn't ask for a better father. I don't think it's possible. I want to say thank you for everything that you have done. Not only for myself but for

what you've done for my brother & my mom. You mean the world to all of us. I know things have been for all you guys & I'm sorry for that. But this is my job & what I live for. I know that you understand that. When I get home, I would like to go up north, just me and you, like before I left & go hunting or canoeing, depending on the weather & I can't wait to look at the 'vette & understand things finally. We'll compare mechanic scars! Well, just remember, you're the best Dad in the world!
Have a Merry Christmas & a Happy New Year!

Love always,
Holly
2003

And another one to her brother.

Robert,
Hi, Robbie. How are you doing! Just wanted to say that I do miss you. Hope you like your radio. Remember, I get to borrow your car when I get back & I'll drink a little with ya at my party (don't tell Mom, Dad, okay). I hope you've been keeping up the good work in school. Everyone has been real proud of you. Hopefully I'll be back no later than *April! You take care & stay out of trouble, don't make the same mistakes I did! But have fun being a teenager! Take care of Mom & Dad!*
Have a Merry Christmas & a Happy New Year!

Love Always,
Your Big Sister,
Holly
2003

It seemed that Holly couldn't get enough of her life as a soldier. She was constantly volunteering to go on missions or raids. Often when she wasn't selected, she would stow away. That was the only way Holly got into trouble over in Iraq—by trying to do too much work. (Her most common complaint was that she had too many fathers telling her what to do.)

Her parents could tell that she truly enjoyed her work and the company of her fellow soldiers. In one e-mail, she told her mom about a practical joke she played on some of her buddies.

> *. . . It was pouring last night, so everything was wet today. We had to go pick the people up from the BSA [brigade support area]. I was leading and I drove right past the road. It was really dark (don't worry; it wasn't anything like the Jessica Lynch thing). So I turned around and found the drive. Then I went to slow down when I was going through a puddle, and my platoon sergeant said to "get me some," so I sped up and just went straight through the puddle. I totally drenched everyone in the back of my truck. They were all luckily laughing their asses off. It was really, really funny. Me and Sgt. Pitts were even laughing (he's my Plt. Sgt.; I'm his driver) so we were all cracking up about the whole thing. So it was actually a good day. Hopefully tomorrow is a good day too.*

In another correspondence, she spoke of teaching Iraqi children to play Duck, Duck, Goose! even though they didn't speak a word of English. Much to Paula's delight, Holly occasionally found time on the weekends to instant message with her mother. Those conversations were almost always filled with girl talk about Holly's new love interest, a soldier by the name of Sergio Cardenas.

Holly and Sergio had met about four months earlier, when her unit moved into the camp where he was stationed. Their first meeting was an accidental encounter.

"I thought she was somebody else," Sergio says. "I just started talking to her. Then I realized she wasn't who I thought it was. But we kept talking."

The infantry specialist from Weslaco, Texas, soon found he had a lot in common with Holly. They both liked action movies; they loved to watch Holly's favorite flick, *Bad Boys*, together. She always gave him a hard time about Michigan football teams beating Texas teams. Sergio remembers that Holly was always up for whatever came along, whether it was casual horseplay between soldiers or a dangerous mission.

Holly did face many harrowing situations. One e-mail she wrote her parents on January 5, 2004, describes the constant concerns Holly and her troops had about improvised explosive devices (IEDs), which were any form of homemade bomb.

MONDAY, JAN. 5. 2004
Hi, you guys. What's going on on that side of the world? Things are OK over here. Today when my section rolled out of the gate we saw someone drop a can on the ground, and we thought it was an IED. So I stopped right away and backed up. We got out and pulled security. Then we called Charlie Co. out to take a look. Well, it ended up not being an IED. I felt a little embarrassed, but at the same time I knew that we had done the right thing. And I have full confidence in the people I work with—if they felt anybody's life was in danger, they would do everything in their power not to let anything happen.

Anyway, that was the most exciting thing that happened today—so far. Everything here is good and I'm doing good. I am very thankful for having such a caring and loving family! I really can't wait to get home. I can't wait to see everyone. I really miss you all soooooo much—if it weren't for you guys, I would have never been able to make it through all this.

But through it all, Holly kept her spirits high and her love for her country strong. She was proud of what she was doing in Iraq, a fact that's evident in the e-mail she wrote to her Little Grams and Pappa on January 9, 2004.

We are so close to coming home. The more and more people I talk to, they all keep making me think that we will for sure be home by April, at the latest. What is really cool is that if we are in the country still on April 1, I will get my 2nd set of combat stripes—one for the first 6 months, and my 2nd will be for the next 6 months I was here. I still can't believe that I'm only 19 and had my combat patch when I was 18. To me, that makes me feel very proud of my life. What's even cooler is that I will be only 20 years old when I do get out. That's very young and I will have already accomplished so much in my life. Cool, huh? Then I'm definitely gonna sit back and relax and go to college. Then I'm coming back as an officer, but only after I have some fun at college. Well, I'm gonna get off now cuz my hands are getting really cold, but you guys take care. Love you guys lots and miss you guys a whole bunch.

Love, Holly

Holly and a fellow soldier in Tikrit, Iraq

McGEOGH FAMILY COLLECTION

The last day of January 2004—the day before she was to be promoted to Specialist—Private, First Class Holly J. McGeogh volunteered for another mission. She had to drive a Humvee sixty miles to Kirkuk to pick up some truck parts. Corporal Juan C. Cabralbanuelos, a twenty-five-year-old from Emporia, Kansas, and Sergeant Eliu Miersandoval, twenty-seven, of San Clemente, California, were with her, along with several other vehicles in the convoy traveling down the macadam road. Holly's Humvee was bringing up the rear: her vehicle was equipped with an MK-19 grenade launcher. In the case of an ambush, she would use that firepower to protect the rest of the vehicles traveling ahead of her.

Suddenly, an IED detonated, ripping through the bottom of the vehicle and sending shrapnel spewing in every direction. The blast created a crater that was two feet deep and four feet wide. Other than the twisted frame, there wasn't a single piece of the Humvee left that was bigger than a dinner plate. The fiery explosion threw Holly over two hundred yards from her vehicle, tossed her helmet off her head, and burst open her body armor. A field report would later detail that the bones in her face were severely broken. Sergeant Miersandoval and Corporal Cabralbanuelos were also instantly killed.

Back in Taylor, it was a quiet winter Saturday—Super Bowl weekend. Everyone was scurrying about, preparing parties and plans for the next day's game when a man arrived at the door.

"I will never forget that man's face," Paula still says. "I could pick it out of a crowd of a million because I see his face every night."

He was the soldier sent to deliver the notification that Holly had been killed in action on a road near Tikrit.

Paula remembers thinking, "if I don't let him in . . . he can't tell me . . ." But deep down, she already knew what he was going to say.

"I need to speak to you," he told her firmly.

The family that had been planning a homecoming celebration suddenly had to start planning a funeral.

As the tragic news spread, Holly's house filled up with people. The phone rang nonstop. At Truman High School, word of Holly's death shook the hallways where she had roamed so carefree two years earlier. Particularly grief stricken were the students that were enrolled in the JROTC. Many knew Holly from the days she had served and considered her their mentor and leader.

When Holly's body returned home, a funeral mass was held at Saint Joseph Catholic Church in Wyandotte. Hundreds had turned out for the nineteen-year-old's funeral. The procession, which consisted of more than 130 cars, weaved its way from the church to Our Lady of Hope Cemetery in Brownstown Township. As the hearse carrying her flag-draped casket passed a group of construction workers, they stopped, removed their hats, and lowered their heads in tribute. One stranger got out of his car and placed his hand over his heart as Private, First Class McGeogh passed by for the last time.

At the cemetery, First Sergeant David Cress, wearing his dress green uniform, pulled a silver trumpet to his lips and played taps for the fallen soldier, which was followed by a twenty-one-gun salute. Soldiers folded the flag that covered her coffin and presented it to Paula, along with the Purple Heart and Bronze Star her "brave little soldier" had earned.

Afterward, Holly's parents got a letter from her platoon sergeant that gave them a firsthand glimpse at Holly's time in Iraq. Sergeant Gregory Pitt's words brought them great comfort.

To the McGeogh Family and Friends:

First of all I would like to say that I am sorry for your loss. SPC McGeogh was my driver for A17/F. Her call sign was A37D; she took pride in her truck, which was a gunship truck that carried an MK-19, which is a very powerful piece of equipment. SPC McGeogh was kind, sweet, funny, and the most outrageous person I have ever met. She was something special. She was so freehearted. She always spoke of you; she would always say, "My mom is the coolest mom in the world." Her favorite saying was "get you some." She was really a tough little stud. She conducted some raids with the infantry guys, because they had to search females. She was so happy to go out and feel a part of the team. SPC McGeogh contributed so much to these soldiers in this company. Whatever she had, if you needed it, she would give it to you. She always would make me laugh when we would be on patrols, conducting missions. She always wore her dark military glasses, which made her eye straight. But around dark-light hours, she would always have a hard time seeing because she left her clear glasses back at the task force support area. I would tell her that she was doing an outstanding job driving and that I had her back. SPC McGeogh had grown to be a wonderful mechanic, which I always admired about her. Even though the army would let female soldiers choose those types of jobs, when they arrived to a unit, the female mechanics would often get stuck in the orderly room doing paperwork. But not SPC McGeogh. She was out on the line with the guys, changing engines, transmissions, changing starters and everything else. Your daughter will forever have a spot in my heart. I will truly miss her. You and her friends will forever be in our prayers and thoughts. If my wife, Kim, and I can do anything for the McGeogh family, we are here for your assistance.

NO ONE LEFT BEHIND, NO ONE IS FORGOTTEN!

Gregory Jerome Pitts
SSG, USA
Platoon Sergeant

Months later, people were still recognizing what Holly did, what she stood for, and what she believed in. In August 2004, Paula found a note on her truck that read, "Sorry for your loss of Holly. I will say a prayer and thank you for all you've done." It was just one of hundreds of notes, letters, and cards that arrived at her home in the year after Holly's death. Many of the notes of gratitude for her daughter's service were unsigned or anonymously signed, "an American."

"People look at me and say I'm strong and that I'm doing a good job," Paula says. "But look at the support we have received. How could I not be strong? Besides, my daughter would be kicking me in the butt if I weren't. I have to be at least half as brave and half as strong as she was."

Those cards, notes, and letters provided comfort to Paula. "People just want to send me condolences, let me know they are thinking of me, praying for Holly, for us. They want us to know how grateful they are for my daughter. They are pretty much thanking me for raising my daughter the way I did," she says.

Holly once said something that her mother will never forget.

"I am so grateful to have grown up in the United States. The freedom we have is wonderful. You see the kids in Iraq, it is very, very sad to see them starving, always begging."

She shared some of her Twizzlers with those hungry kids.

Specialist Sergio Cardenas was out on another mission the day Holly died. He did not return until late in the evening. When he got back to camp, a sergeant pulled him aside to tell him the terrible news.

"Are you sure?" he remembers asking.

"Yes, it was Holly," was the reply.

Sergio knows that he will never forget Holly, whom he affectionately called "my little wrench monkey" or "my baby." She was more than just another soldier. She was bright and energetic, and always traveled with a smile on her face. And she always went after what she wanted.

"I told her not to go out of the gates for any reason," Sergio emphatically says, remembering countless conversations he had with Holly. "I told her not to volunteer, not to put her hand up."

But on that fateful day, she did, as she had done so many times before. Holly McGeogh knew no fear.

Three days before she died, she sent her last correspondence home to her parents. The poignant e-mail embodies everything that Holly was in life. She was an energetic teenage girl whose head was filled with visions of romance, but she was also a tough soldier and mechanic serving her country in the harsh Iraqi desert. If she hadn't volunteered for that last mission to Kirkuk, she would be alive today. But that just wouldn't have been Holly. In the end, it would take a bomb to shatter the dreams and aspirations of young Private, First Class McGeogh.

> *Hey you guys, it's been a long time since I have written, sorry. Well, we have to go to the BSA [brigade support area]. It's alright I guess. I hate the fact that I can't see Sergio. I miss him soooooo much. I have been on this cleanup detail where we have been going back and forth from the palace and the BSA. Today when I was getting ready to come back over, my friend Karen was on the radio, and someone said hi. I was like "what?" and she said, "It's your baby." So he was there where I live when I was getting ready to leave, and I couldn't even get to talk to him. Mom, this is truly breaking my heart cuz I can't see him. He really means a lot to me. He should be at the BSA around the 20th of Feb. hopefully. I just want to give him a huge hug and kiss. Well, I should stop talking about him but it all just pisses me off. So what all has been going on back home? I just found out that our flight dates are March 23–28, so hopefully everything goes as planned. The days have been going by sorta fast, but knock on wood. I don't want them to start going by slow. I'm gonna try to go on the Internet tonight. I just gotta see how things go tonight. Well, how is everyone? I still haven't gotten my*

speakers yet. Can you check on them? I finally got my earpieces today for my radios. Well, I think I am gonna end this for now. I'll try to write again real soon. I love and miss you guys sooooo much. I promise I'll be safe.

Love, Holly

ONWARD, CHRISTIAN SOLDIER

Thank you so much for everything you guys do for me. Please eat some pernil, drink some tequila, and have lots of fun for me this Christmas! I miss y'all so much and I cannot wait to have our own celebration when I get home. I love y'all!*

—CAPTAIN ERNESTO BLANCO

You can be sure of one thing: if Ernesto M. Blanco were alive today, he would be making music.

He would be playing his Spanish guitar and singing one of his favorite songs. He would be wearing an old pair of boots and a white cowboy hat, sitting in the shade under a tree and strumming. He might even have a beer by his side. A devout Presbyterian, Ernie didn't see anything wrong with drinking in moderation. Celebrating life with music, joy, and the occasional drink was very much a part of his faith.

"Ernie had such a beautiful voice. You didn't have to ask him twice

*a Puerto Rican dish consisting mainly of a pork roast shoulder.

At home in San Antonio, enjoying a beer
BLANCO FAMILY COLLECTION

to sing, ever," his sister Carmen Pendergraff recalls. It never mattered where he was, or whom he was with.

"He would perform anywhere. He would know you for twenty seconds and then pull out his guitar and play for you."

He used to say, "I don't believe life is just a waiting room for heaven."

Ernie came into the world eight weeks early. His mother, Gloria Blanco, had to rush back to Hartford, Connecticut, from New York City (where she was seeing a show) when she realized her son was going to arrive before she had planned.

"He was just in a hurry to be born," she says. In a hurry, it seems in retrospect, to start enjoying life.

After his birth in 1975, Ernie's parents moved to San Juan, Puerto Rico, where their young son flourished. By the time he was two and a half, Ernie was showing signs of musical inclination. He could strum a Spanish acoustical guitar before he could hold it. Soon, he was singing along with the chords he taught himself to play.

When he wasn't playing his guitar or singing, Ernie was playing baseball or simply running barefoot in the warm San Juan breezes. He was always smiling.

"He made friends right away," Gloria said. "And that was scary when he was so small. He would talk to anyone."

As his natural talent became more and more evident, he received classical instruction on the guitar. His parents were always there to support his love of music, whether it was in the setting of a formal concert or an impromptu performance around the living-room table.

Ernie's first career aspiration was to be an astronaut. His parents sent him to the Space Camp Florida Training Center, located near NASA's Kennedy Space Center. Afterwards, his mother says, "He wore his jumpsuit constantly for about a month."

When he was fifteen, Ernie's parents divorced and he moved with his mother and sister to San Antonio, Texas. Not surprisingly, he fit right in. He loved the influence Latino culture had on the city.

"He immediately fell in love with Texas," Gloria recalls. "The minute he hit the ground here, he knew he was home. He went from being Ernesto Blanco to Ernie Blanco, wearing cowboy boots and learning how to country dance."

Always industrious, Ernie started working at a car wash after school and in the summer. With his outgoing personality, quick smile, and friendly manner, he earned healthy tips.

He started using his popularity to forward the only other cause in his life greater than his love of music: God. Ernie formed a small ministry that operated out of the car wash. He was ready to talk about scripture to anyone who would listen.

Following his graduation from Churchill High School in 1993, Ernie enrolled at Texas A&M. He loved everything about the Aggie college life, from country music to Tex-Mex food to Shiner Bock Beer to Texas girls. He earned the nickname Energizer Bunny for his never-ending supply of enthusiasm. His mother remembers too that "he was always in love."

Ernie worked hard both in class and out. He enrolled in A&M's ROTC program. As a Ross Volunteer, an honor he earned with the Corps of Cadets, he welcomed the Texas governor, then George W.

Bush. He applied himself in his academic studies and did well in school.

In 1998, after he graduated from A&M, Ernie Blanco-Caldas joined the military. (Even after his parents divorced, Ernie would often include his mother's maiden name, Caldas, in his surname as a sign of respect.) He had come to believe that service was a crucial part of fully appreciating the blessings and privileges of living in the United States—in fact, he thought it should be a requirement for all men to serve. His goal was to become a member of the famed 82nd Airborne. Ernie's relatives had served in the 82nd with distinction, and he wanted to follow the family tradition. After officer training, he volunteered and was accepted into the prestigious unit.

Ernie quickly became a second lieutenant platoon leader at Fort Bragg, North Carolina.

Every now and then, Gloria visited her son. She was constantly chagrined by the state of his bachelor's apartment. Some of Ernie's old college habits had stuck with him. He never did laundry. When he ran out of clean underwear, he just bought more at Kmart, which added to the ever-growing pile of dirty clothes until his mom arrived and washed them for him.

"He was very busy, leaving before 5:00 a.m. and working until 10:00 p.m.," she says in his defense.

Ernie took his duty as a soldier very seriously and his dedication left little time for housekeeping. There were times that he had to simply drop everything and leave.

"I'll be off the radar for a couple of weeks," he would tell his mother. That was the signal that he was going on a training exercise.

After September 11, 2001, Ernie knew the 82nd Airborne was likely to deploy. He was convinced that because of the success of the 9/11 attacks, more strikes were soon to follow.

"We have to take the fight to them," he told his mother. "If we don't take the war to them, then we will be fighting them in the streets of San Antonio."

The 82nd Airborne deployed to Afghanistan only a few days after the Twin Towers fell. But even in the face of danger, Ernie kept his heart and his mind open. He became absolutely enamored of the people of Afghanistan.

"The people were wonderful," he exclaimed to his mother.

On Wednesdays Ernie would lead some of his fellow soldiers in a Bible study group. And of course, he was often to be found strumming his guitar and singing.

By the time Ernie returned home in February of 2003, a woman named Michelle Sorrel was back in his life. The two had first met in college in 1999, when Ernie's roommate was dating Michelle's roommate.

"Because our roommates were dating and we were both teaching a Bible study in the college class at Grace Bible Church [College Station, Texas], we spent a lot of time together," Michelle explains. "We became really close friends and wanted to date, but the timing wasn't right."

Ernie, then 24, had already graduated, but was working in College Station. Meanwhile, a twenty-one-year-old Michelle was still in school, with two more years to go before earning her B.A. in English. Soon after they met, Ernie was sent to Officer Candidate School.

"The timing was just never right for us, largely because we were usually 1,000 miles apart (or more) and I was still in college," Michelle recalls.

Ernie and Michelle kept in touch, and saw each other whenever they could. But all that changed in July of 2003. Ernie came back to San Antonio to visit his father and stepmother, Jose and Thaimi Blanco. As soon as he got into town, he called Michelle.

"We got together for dinner and spent most of the next week together," she recalls. "We knew that the time was right. This was it!"

Herself a woman of deep faith, Michelle was the perfect match for Ernie. She says now, "it was then that we knew it was finally God's timing for our relationship."

The next few months were exciting for the couple. They filled their days together with their mutual passions: Texas two-step dancing, guitar playing and singing, quiet times alone with each other, and scripture study.

"Ernie and I both loved studying scripture," Michelle says. "He had the wonderful opportunity of doing a Bible study with some of his men [in the military]. For a Christian, the Bible is an incredibly precious gift. It is intimacy with our Savior. It is the very Word of God, and Ernie and I both treasured ours."

Then, Ernie found out that his unit was deploying to Iraq. Before he left, he asked the pretty Michelle to marry him. She said yes.

"We knew before he left that we wanted to get married when he returned. We were so tired of being apart, and couldn't wait to be together," she says.

Ernie playing his guitar

BLANCO FAMILY COLLECTION

Like Michelle, Gloria was only looking forward to the time when her son would return home. She recalls something she said to Michelle in Ft. Bragg, the weekend before Ernie deployed:

"I remember commenting to Michelle as we watched those beautiful young men and women all spruced up in their starched fatigues, that some of these folks would not be coming back. I never imagined that Ernie would be one of them."

The duties of Ernie's Iraq command with the 1st Battalion, 504th Parachute Infantry Regiment were stressful. His division was positioned in a dangerous location, a hot spot of insurgency near Qaryat Ash Shababi. His job, which included overseeing support and transport missions for his battalion, was always perilous—as a leader, Ernie was always on the front lines.

But true to form, Ernie made the best of his situation. The Texas flag he kept by his bunk brought him comforting thoughts of home. He kept in close contact with his mother, primarily through e-mails, often asking her to send him beef jerky and Handi Wipes (since bathing facilities were scarce). He also requested that she keep him updated on the latest Texas news, particularly the fortunes of his beloved San Antonio Spurs.

Ernie was only able to call Michelle once a week, for about 10 minutes. (He usually phoned late Monday nights, between 12:30 a.m. and 3 a.m.) But it was clear that his fiancée never left his mind. One time, as a surprise, he ordered a beautiful yellow miniature rosebush as well as a box of Godiva chocolates on the Internet, and had them delivered to her. Ernie also purchased her Christmas present on-line, and had it shipped to Michelle's mother's house so that she would have his present under the tree on Christmas morning. His gift was a pair of Roper boots for Michelle to wear when the couple went out two-stepping.

In early December, 2003, Ernie found time to write a quick note to his Shell (his nickname for Michelle):

> *"I hope you are doing well. Hun, the time seems to be going by so fast, yet it seems to be dragging. I cannot explain it, but it just seems to be that way . . . Thoughts of you keep me sane in this place."*
>
> *"Shell, I want you to know that you are in my thoughts at all times . . . I truly cannot wait to spend time with you."*

Ernie didn't let the distance between him and his fiancée prevent him from helping to plan his wedding. He asked a chaplain friend from Fort Bragg to marry the couple the following summer.

"We hoped to be married by June so that we could move to Fort Benning, Georgia where he could attend the Advanced Course," Michelle says.

Ernie entrusted his mother, Gloria, with a very special wedding mission.

He had come across a Web site that allowed customers to design their own engagement rings. He gave his mother a budget and a specific design and started her on a quest to find a ring worthy of his Shell.

Ernie carried his Christian mission forward by continuing to hold weekly Bible study meetings. He didn't see any problem with being both a soldier and a Christian. He would say that he was just honoring the Lord by doing the job he was called to do. The fellowship Ernie led was stamped with his characteristic love of life—something easy to see in an e-mail he wrote to his fiancée in November 2003:

> *Here is a list of some of my favorite things (in no particular order): Michelle (this one is!); hanging out with family; country music; rock & roll (or any music with guitar in it); the sound of a steel guitar and fiddles; dancing (especially at Gruene Hall or John T. Flores); food (especially Puerto Rican,*

Mexican, and any kind of seafood); being outside; horses; studying scripture and theology; any water sport; learning to be like Christ; life; wine and beer (especially Shiner!); Texas (and everything that comes with it); rodeo; my friends; driving and road trips; cowboy stuff; dogs; the country and ranches; being a soldier; forgiveness and grace; reading; guitar playing; songs; live music; driving up 281 and around the Texas hill country (especially Luckenbach); worship; church (THE Church); fellowship; baseball games; football; the Aggies (and being one); campfires; bar-b-que (the real Texas type); Dr. Pepper and big red Motorcycles (Harleys); trucks (Ford F-150 types); freedom in Christ Movies . . .

Honey, you know how I love enjoying the life that God has blessed me with. I enjoy every aspect of His creation. I don't believe life is just a waiting room for heaven. I believe God has intended life to be enjoyed by His creatures and I intend to enjoy it. Honey, I like to listen to loud music, dance in smokey dance halls, drink a few beers, hang out with my family and friends and just have a good time! After seeing the things I've seen here, I realize that life is just too short not to live 100%. I understand the need to preach the Gospel not just through words, but also through the very essence of our lives. Jesus, from what I understand from studying John, didn't live halfway. He did everything 100%, to the glory of God.

Ernie spread love and happiness wherever he went. On Christmas Day, 2003, he traded his cowboy hat in for a Santa hat and took a stroll around the camp.

Sgt. Bart Barcelon of Company D later described the scene. "Christmas morning I got stitches in my hand. As I sat there getting stitched up, in walks Ernie with his Santa Claus hat on, walking around the base spreading cheer."

Ernie stopped to talk to the sergeant. "He told me and the medic about the engagement ring he had just gotten and asked us for suggestions for a honeymoon location. After being assured that I was okay, he left to go spread more cheer and happiness throughout the base in a depressing time."

On December 28, 2003, Ernie was killed when an improvised explosive device hit his vehicle in Qaryat Ash Shababi, Iraq. He was performing a support mission with the HHC scouts of the 82nd Airborne Division. Three other soldiers who were in the truck survived the attack.

On the day of her parents' fifty-eighth wedding anniversary, Gloria stopped by the condo where she, Ernie, and her parents had lived together for a while (where her parents were still living). When she walked into their living room, prepared to drop off the gift she had purchased, she saw two uniformed soldiers sitting on the sofa. One was a sergeant; the other was a chaplain.

"Are you Gloria Caldas?" the sergeant asked.

"Yes."

"Are you the mother of Captain Ernesto M. Blanco-Caldas?"

"Yes."

The sergeant took a deep breath and started reading.

"The Secretary of Defense regrets to inform you of the death of your son . . ."

His words faded out of Gloria's mind as she started shaking her head.

"I couldn't believe it," she says. "I couldn't keep it together. I fell apart."

Years before, when his parents divorced, Ernie told his mother that he would never do anything that would make her cry.

He had managed to keep his promise for so many years. But not forever.

Ernie had always told his mother that he wanted to be buried in San Antonio, the place he considered his true home. So, on January 7, 2004, just ten days after the explosion that took his life, a horse-drawn caisson carried Ernie's flag-draped coffin into Fort Sam Houston National Cemetery. Members of Ernie's adored Eighty-second Airborne served as his pallbearers. To date, Ernie is the highest-ranking Texan that has been killed in the war against terrorism. Over four hundred people paid their last respects at his funeral.

Standing by the grave next to Ernie's mother and sister was the woman who would have been his wife. Later, Michelle would recall how often she and Ernie had talked about their future together. Ernie had been considering pursuing a medical career in the army, but what he really wanted to do was to pursue his passion for Christ.

"He really wanted to go the RTS, Reformed Theological Seminary, in Florida," Michelle remembers. "If, at some point, he decided to finish his career in the army, seminary would most likely have been the direction he would have gone next. He had a real gift for teaching, and loved the Lord very much. We talked about his working in the youth ministry and someday becoming a pastor. We had yet to see how God would unfold our lives."

The couple talked about one day owning a ranch with horses. "We eventually wanted to come back to Texas and raise our family here. We looked forward to having a family."

In one of his last written communications, Ernie sent a quick e-mail to his fiancée. The message was short, but it said everything:

Shell,
You are everything to me. Thoughts of you are the smile on my lips. I find it hard to put into words how much I love you. I cannot wait to come home to you! I love you!

Love,
Ernie

Michelle Sorrel, now a 7th grade History/English teacher at Trinity Christian Academy in Addison, Texas, still wears the diamond ring Ernie chose for her before he died. He had told his stepmother, Thaimi, that it would be the ring Michelle would wear for the rest of her life.

In his twenty-eight years on Earth, Ernie touched many people, with both his music and his love of Jesus.

"He was amazing. He made everyone feel special, and he made me feel like I was the best mom in the world. My heart was and still is broken," Gloria says.

His sister Carmen adds, "Everyone that knew him felt like they were Ernie's favorite, and that is a great gift."

Soldiers remember him for both his songs and his Bible teachings. Many have said that Ernie led others to Jesus, both before and after his death. A second lieutenant that served under Ernie commented on an online memorial site, "Everyone remembers his smile and his love of the Lord." He added that Ernie "gave me his first lieutenant bars when he made captain, and I shall wear them with honor when I get promoted. It is hard here without him, but he is with Jesus and smiling all the time . . . Even in his death, the Lord continues to work through his memory and lead people to Christ, which I think is what makes Ernie smile the most."

Though his music has been silenced, the words that truly defined his life—the words that are carved into his grave marker—ring forever clear.

"I have kept the faith."

Ernie's last correspondence home consists of a series of e-mail exchanges between him and his mother on December 24, 2003. Reading them, one is left to wonder how much more love, happiness, and

Ernie and Michelle

PHOTO PROVIDED BY MICHELLE SORREL

spirit Ernie Blanco could have brought into the world had his life not been cut short.

Mom-
Thank you so much for everything you guys do for me. Please eat some pernil, drink some tequila, and have lots of fun for me this Christmas! I miss y'all so much and I cannot wait to have our own celebration when I get home. I love y'all!
Ernie

Hi, baby! Can't eat the pernil (my cholesterol's too high), can't drink the tequila (my liver's shot), but I will remember you every second during these holidays!
Mom

Mom-
Quick question. Since we will probably have a short time to plan a wed-

ding, I was thinking on possibilities for a rehearsal dinner (since it is the groom's family's responsibility :)).

Shell and I will probably be married in the D/FW area and I was thinking we could have the rehearsal dinner at Billy Bob's!

They have a party room and good barbecue and after dinner we can all dance the night away!

What do you think?

Ernie

Honey . . . Sounds like too much fun! I love Fort Worth and I don't think it would be too much trouble to plan!

Economical, too!

Mommy

I'm glad you think it would be cool. Apparently they have some really nice rooms that they can set up for the events. I'm pretty pumped!

Hi, Honey:

I went out to their Web site and saw the rooms they have available. They are too cool! I think the most important thing, though, is for Michelle and you to set the date, make arrangements for the church and reception, and then verify that the venue is available for the rehearsal dinner. What does Michelle think? Have you discussed this with her?

Mom

Yes, I have discussed it with her and she thinks it's very cool!

Ernie

A Twenty-Third Birthday Present

Thanks Dad, for everything. I love you and miss you.

—SERGEANT JUSTIN WRISLEY GARVEY

There is a special bond between father and son. It cannot be broken or shattered, even as both grow older or are separated by hundreds and thousands of miles. Justin and Gregg Garvey had such a connection.

In retrospect, it's not hard to see why they grew so close. When Justin was only fifteen months old, his dad was already pitching him balls. The toddler showed a knack for swinging a bat and making contact. (Years later, when Justin was in high school, he'd play third base on the varsity team.)

When a bond is that strong, certain moments are bound to stand out like snapshots in a father's mind. There was the day when the elder Garvey poured cement at his produce stand. Gregg grabbed his infant son and plunked his feet in the soupy gray mix, forever immortalizing a year-old Justin. There were memories of some of those early soccer practices with Coach Garvey at the helm. It seemed that every

Gregg and Justin Garvey on the Fourth of July, 1980

PHOTO BY GREGG GARVEY

new activity, and every passing day, brought father and son closer together.

There was only one factor in Justin's young life that came close to rivaling the influence that his father had, and that was the military base close to the Garvey home. When his mother, Angie Perkett Garvey, delivered Justin on February 29, 1980, little did she or Gregg dream that there, in her arms, was a future sergeant in the United States Army. But as it turned out, the base would have a profound affect on the younger Garvey as he grew from a playful boy to an adolescent. Justin loved to watch the soldiers as they trained and stood in awe of their example.

After Justin's parents separated, he moved with his mother to Proctor, Vermont, a sleepy little hamlet southwest of Montpelier, tucked away just inside the New York–Vermont border. There, his natural leadership skills ripened. He became the captain of his high school's soccer team. He was a good student, earning A's and never missing classes.

It was during his junior year that Justin made the big decision: he joined the National Guard when he was seventeen. And he stuck with it. Ten days after graduating from Proctor High School, Jason arrived at Fort Benning, Georgia, to begin his basic training.

"Well, Dad, if I don't do it now, I will never do it," Jason said, as he explained his decision to his father.

Although it was a far cry from what he was used to, the hot and humid weather in Georgia didn't deter Justin. In fact, he thrived in the new environment. By carefully watching his instructors and pushing himself in the precision training, Justin turned into a model soldier, which wasn't surprising to anyone, least of all his father. After all, Justin used to tell everybody when he was growing up that he "wanted to be a pilot and fly around and protect my country." And though Justin returned home to New England for a few years to work in an oil company, in 1999 he decided to leave the National Guard and return to the army full-time.

Soon Private Garvey was stationed at another Southern base: Fort Campbell, Kentucky. It didn't take long for Justin to impress his commanders there. He followed orders and directions well and always was an example for his peers. Justin earned his place in the army's famed 101st Airborne, the gallant paratrooper unit from World War II.

At his father's house in Florida, Easter 2002

PHOTO BY GREGG GARVEY

It was during Justin's time at Fort Campbell that America suffered through the horror of 9/11.

Three days later, on September 14, 2001, the president toured the still-smoking site of the World Trade Center. He spent an hour looking at the devastation, watching as hundreds of rescue workers and firefighters worked with hope and determination, still believing that they might be able to save someone trapped in the massive pile of rubble. The president's presence briefly stopped the excavation process. A downpour had settled the concrete dust that was a miserable irritant to the workers' eyes and throats. For a moment, the air was still and everyone was quiet.

Standing in the rubble, his arm resting on a fireman's shoulder, President Bush spoke through a bullhorn. As he addressed the volunteers, someone yelled out that they could not hear him. The president replied, "I hear you. The rest of the world hears you. And the people who knocked these buildings down will hear from all of us soon."

The president's plan for the country—his plan for men like Justin—had been set into motion. The 101st Airborne received deployment orders. Communications were shut down at the Kentucky base. No calls from or to the soldiers were allowed. In the middle of it all was twenty-one-year-old Private Justin Wrisley Garvey. Without saying good-bye to his family, he slipped away during the darkness of a Kentucky night with his unit.

"I knew that he knew, and he knew that I knew, that we were not going to let the bastards get away with it," Gregg says. Garvey explains that he knew where his son had been sent, despite the lack of any official word.

As the days passed and the smoke cleared in lower Manhattan, hope dimmed that any survivors were going to be found in the rubble of the World Trade Center towers. However, workers continued to dig deeper.

Halfway around the world, Justin was digging too—a deep trench in the rocky soil of Afghanistan. Deployed to a remote and barren section of the country, Justin's duty was simple: protect his fellow soldiers by positioning and operating a mortar, laying down firepower on anyone that encroached on their position. Justin had mastered the use of the mortar (a tubelike weapon that fires small bombs dropped in from the top) in training in Kentucky. A relatively simple and easily transportable weapon, the mortar was capable of producing substantial destruction, especially in the hands of an expert like Justin. His prowess and dedication to his job did not go unnoticed by his commanders. Justin received a field promotion to corporal.

A painful hernia sent Corporal Garvey back to Fort Campbell in 2002. In some ways, the injury was a blessing for his father. As his body mended, Justin was able to spend some time with Gregg in Florida. Their father-son bond grew even stronger.

During that time, Justin got another piece of good news: he received word that he had been promoted to sergeant. Loyal to his troops to the end, he opted not to wear the third stripe until his men returned from Afghanistan, so they could witness his receipt of the promotion.

That spring was a busy one for Justin. He asked his high school sweetheart, Kate Garner, to marry him. On June 1, 2002, the kid that was now a veteran of military action in Afghanistan married Katie. The newlyweds moved back to Oak Grove, Kentucky, near the army fort.

By the time February of 2003 rolled around, Justin was putting in long hours of training at the base. He left his home at 4:45 a.m. and did not return until 7:30 p.m. Gregg knew what the arduous hours meant: once again, the 101st Airborne was about to deploy, this time to Iraq.

He spoke to Justin twice on his twenty-third birthday that year.

An hour and a half after their first conversation, Justin called his dad back to say, "Hey dad, guess what the army just gave me for my twenty-third birthday?"

"What?" the elder Garvey asked, already knowing what the answer would be.

"An all-expense-paid trip to Iraq," Sergeant Garvey replied.

By March, Sergeant Garvey and his men, Headquarters Company, 1-187 Infantry Battalion, were stationed near Mosul, Iraq. There was steady work, including patrols and rescue missions. (Much of what Justin did still remains classified.) But as spring turned to summer, a very important date approached. July 18 was the day when Justin's voluntary commitment to the army would be over.

He had a choice to make: he could return to civilian life and his wife Katie, or reenlist. Both choices would involve leaving his active unit in Iraq. By that time, he had qualified to become a warrant officer and fly helicopters. If he reenlisted, he would head for a yearlong training program. When he graduated, he would be a chopper pilot, something he had dreamed about since he was a child.

But if he went home, he could spend time with his beloved wife. It was a difficult decision for Sergeant Garvey, one that he put off making even as he took on the responsibility of training his replacement as the important date approached. He was torn between two worlds.

The night of July 18, 2003, Justin was resting in a tent, wrestling with the decision he had yet to make, when suddenly a commander appeared asking for volunteers. The mission was simple: deliver a message to some men deployed farther down the road. Loyal to the end, even in his time of indecision, Sergeant Garvey jumped to his feet.

As the vehicle commander, Justin rode in the passenger seat of the Humvee. Sergeant Jason D. Jordan of Elba, Alabama—the man that was to be Justin's replacement—rode along with him. It was late; the last official day of Justin's enlistment was almost over.

Suddenly, without warning, their vehicle was ambushed on a road near Tallifar. An insurgent launched a rocket-propelled grenade into the Humvee. The explosion killed Sergeants Garvey and Jordan.

On July 28, 2003, Sergeant Justin Wrisley Garvey was laid to rest at the Cedar Grove Cemetery in Fair Haven, Vermont, with full military honors. His family watched as his flag-draped coffin was carried to the grave site. His mother, father, brother Adam, sister Kristin, and his wife Katie mourned the loss, along with other relatives and friends. The model soldier from the small New England town had returned home forever.

Sergeant Garvey's military career earned him many honors and awards. He received the Expert Infantryman's Badge, the Combat Infantryman's Badge, and the National Defense Service Medal. He excelled in the Primary Leadership Development Course and the Air Assault School. He was posthumously awarded a Purple Heart and a Bronze Star.

Justin's death was especially hard on his devoted father and Gregg soon realized he had to find an outlet for his grief. "The night of Justin's funeral and into the early morning hours of July 29 I couldn't sleep, so I got up and walked through the downtown of my hometown in New York State. I'd had this idea after the funeral that I just wanted to do more.

"This feeling of helplessness was just overwhelming," Gregg continues. The night of the funeral, he thought of "all the folks that lost their children in this war, in an automobile accident or drowning or whatever. They lost a child, and that's just devastating."

His desire to do something kept working on him over the coming weeks.

"Then it came to me as I was sitting here. I was holding a picture of Justin and was looking at my flagpole out in front of the house. I had this vision of a memorial.

"I had been thinking about what on earth I was going to do with the rest of my life. That's when I made the decision that these memorials were what I was going to do to move on," Gregg explains.

Then an even grander idea hit him.

"I thought, 'You know, the simplicity of this memorial, the basic design, I could put one in the hometown of every hero we lost or will lose in this war."

He conceived of a simple design: a flagpole, the soldier's rifle stuck in the ground bayonet first, and a helmet. Each memorial would include a plain but eloquent plaque with the soldier's name, dates, and service information. Gregg plans to put a memorial in as many towns as he can, starting with his own.

Despite the violent death of Sergeant Garvey, the bond between father and son remains unbroken. Gregg still mourns the loss of his "Hobie"—a nickname he coined years before when Justin played soccer—and finds it difficult to speak of the details of his son's death. But he finds solace in the reverent memorials that he creates. And he knows that his son's sacrifice won't be forgotten.

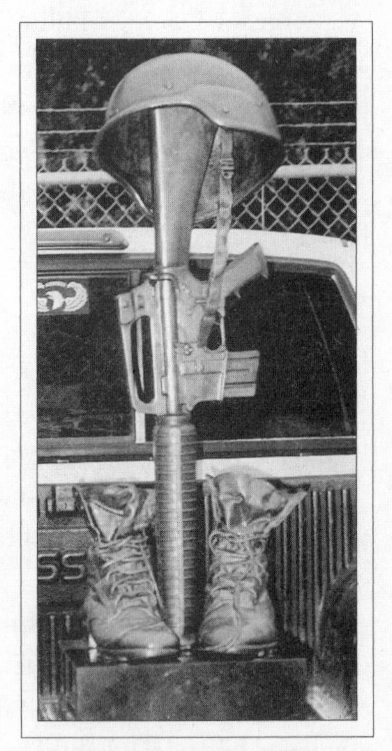

*The Garvey Memorial—
"Lest they be forgotten."*
PHOTO BY GREGG GARVEY

Gregg met with President Bush

when he traveled to Fort Campbell in the spring of 2004 to console families that lost loved ones. He heard from Sergeant Doug Norman, the sole survivor of the ambush that took the lives of Sergeants Garvey and Jordan. Norman was in the Humvee that terrible night in Iraq. He has since been reassigned to the army's Old Guard. Now Sergeant Norman serves with the honor guard assigned to Arlington National Cemetery. His reenlistment was in honor of Sergeants Garvey and Jordan.

"I am honored and overwhelmed and humbled by that," Gregg says.

The last written words Gregg Garvey received from his son are a lasting testament to the unbreakable bond between them.

13 May 03
Dad,
Hi, how are you? I'm pretty good. Not too much going on here now. We have moved from Baghdad, north to a town just west of Mosul, close to the Syrian border. We are now guarding an oil storage facility and propane filling station. Fun, fun. I've taken over a squad, one gun, the same gun as in Pakistan before I got hurt. They are a good group of guys. We picked out a little house kinda by itself, to stay in. It's nicer than the rest. We fixed the windows and put a door on it. One of the Iraqi workers wired in a light for us, and I wired a switch on it today so we can turn it on and off. We have six people staying in it, five from the squad and our interpreter. He's a nice guy and he's Kurdish. They have been fighting against Saddam forever. Don't know how long we will be here. I've heard some rumors that they may allow people who are sixty days from getting out to go home, starting in June. That would be me, so I guess we'll see.

How is everything? Is work good? I hope so. Things here are pretty good, pretty boring though. All we do is pull guard. It's really beautiful here though. With rolling grass covered hills everywhere and a lot of small mountains, all treeless, but still real nice to look at. Much better than the desert. Also it is a little cooler up here. Tell Robin, Kokomo, and

Jake I said hi and I love them. Hope to see you guys soon. Thanks, Dad, for everything. I love you and miss you.

Love,

Justin

P.S. What is A.K.T.? It's on the outside of your card. I've been trying to figure it out, but I can't.

WITCH DOCTOR 11

Try not to worry, things aren't as bad as they seem most of the time. I love you guys.

—SPECIALIST CHRISTOPHER A. GOLBY

On the afternoon of Thursday, January 8, 2004, the crew of Witch Doctor 11, a medevac air team, was in the air near the war-torn city of Fallujah. They were part of 571st Air Ambulance Medical Evacuation Company, and their job was to lift wounded troops out of combat zones. It was dangerous work. The army's UH-60 helicopters were favorite ambush targets for insurgents armed with shoulder-held rocket launchers. Though the Red Cross insignia was supposed to be a symbol of peace and mercy recognized the world over, in Iraq it attracted as many bullets as it deterred.

Mohammed Ahmed al-Jamali, a twenty-seven-year-old Iraqi farmer, recalled hearing the distinctive whoosh of a rocket a little after 2:00 p.m. as he worked in his field about four miles south of Fallujah. He looked up and saw a rocket strike the tail of an army helicopter, which he confirmed was marked with a Red Cross insignia. He watched as the aircraft crashed to the ground and burst into flames. He rushed to the burning debris, but he was too late. Everyone was dead. Everyone including a Pennsylvania native by the name of Christopher Golby.

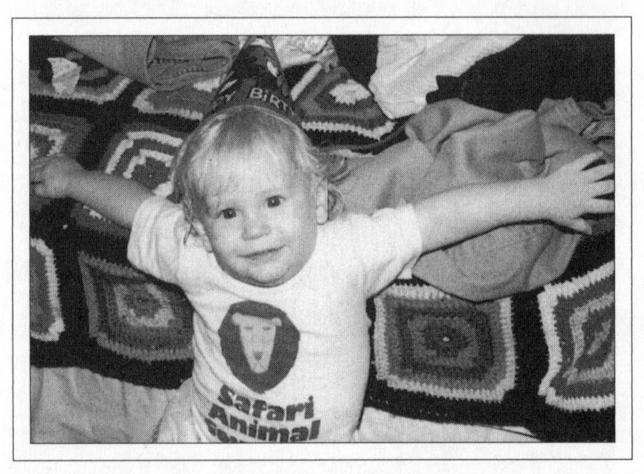

Chris on his 1st birthday

PHOTO BY DAWN GOLBY

From the moment he first put his hands on a helicopter, Chris Golby wanted to fly. That was in high school in Johnston, Pennsylvania, where he was part of the Civil Air Patrol. He soon set his sights on flight school. His mother, Dawn Golby, remembers her son "thought the army would be his ticket into it." When Chris heard about the educational benefits package the army was offering, he didn't waste any more time. He took the test and received a stellar score. When the army promised him a career in aviation, Chris knew his future had officially begun.

Though he was excellent in both basic and flight training, when he got his first job with the military, Chris found himself at the very bottom of the totem pole.

"I pump gas," he told his brother Shane when asked what he did in the army. But the drudgework didn't bother him. He was working around aircraft, and that suited him just fine.

One night, when he was stationed in North Carolina, Chris and his friend Ryan went to a nearby club called Pirates. He spotted a pretty girl walking in and made a promise to his buddy that he would ask her out before the end of the night.

After a few dozen trips to the men's room, Chris gave Sonya a rose he had bought in the club, and his pager number written on a napkin. Then he walked away.

"I paged him the next day," Sonya says. "He ran all the way to the other side of the barracks to call me back." Chris lingered by the phone the rest of the afternoon, hoping to get to talk to her. And his effort didn't go unrewarded: Sonya agreed to accompany him to a carnival.

"We rode rides and played games all night. We talked and got to know one another better. We had a lot of fun," she says. On their second date, they returned to Pirates and played pool and darts.

"We did that as much as we could. I was good at pool and he was good at darts, so we taught one another things. We tried to do things we both liked," Sonya recalls.

As the relationship grew more serious, the two started taking weekend trips to the beach together.

"We liked to take my two boys down there and have fun," she says. (Sonya had two boys, Sean and Jonathan, from a previous marriage.)

On May 13, 1997, Chris and Sonya were wed.

The couple moved overseas when the army stationed Chris at Giebelstadt Army Airfield in Germany, the home of the Twelfth Aviation Brigade and Sixty-ninth Air Defense Artillery Brigade. But neither he nor Sonya minded being away from home. During Chris's off-duty time, he and his wife traveled around the countryside.

"We liked to see all the castles," Sonya recalls.

There were three major Golby family events during their time in Germany. Two were joyous occasions. Chris reenlisted in the army. Then, on December 1, 1998, Sonya gave birth to their son, Dylon.

The third event, by contrast, was one of the darkest days in Chris Golby's life. A close friend of his from basic training was killed in a chopper crash in Kosovo.

"I remember that he was so upset," Sonya says. "He used to tell me that it should've been him that was up there, and not his friend."

Chris was on the mission sent to pick up the dead soldier's body.

"I remember him calling home and saying how hard it was to go and get him and bring him back," Dawn says. "He said that it was the hardest thing he had ever done."

In 2001, the Golbys left Germany and returned to the States. Chris began some new helicopter maintenance training, which took him to Virginia (where he was on that fateful September 11). After a year of training, he requested a post at Fort Carson, Colorado.

He applied for duty with the 571st Air Ambulance. The unit had an illustrious history of combat lifesaving dating back to the earliest generation of "dustoff" pilots. *Dustoff*, a term that refers to the dirt and dust helicopter props stir up on liftoff, had become synonymous with brave and daring helicopter rescue missions that retrieve wounded troops from battlefields under fire.

The 571st was very selective, and admission was far from automatic. But Chris's credentials spoke for themselves. He was chosen for duty as a crew chief.

Making it into the 571st was a seminal event in Chris Golby's life. It dispelled any thought he might have had of leaving the military: "If he could have stayed in the army, doing what he was doing with the 571st, he would never have given it up," his mother says. "He would have stayed there forever."

On March 30, 2003, Chris and his unit deployed to Iraq.

"Chris wasn't afraid," Sonya recalls. "He was looking forward to it. He wanted to help and that is what he did."

As a crew chief, he was responsible for helicopter maintenance. He had the power to ground helicopters if he suspected that they weren't operating properly. On one memorable occasion, Chris grounded all the birds in his fleet, including the commander's chopper. The commander, Major William LaChance, flew into a rage, but Chris stuck by his guns. There was something wrong with each and every UH-60. He simply refused to allow them to fly. Soon, his reputation of being a perfectionist spread. If Chris had worked on a helicopter, there was no doubt that it was in top condition. The flight crews knew his work and trusted it.

Chris threw himself into his work. If there was a mission to do, he would volunteer to be part of it. His commander admitted there were times that he had to ground Chris because he was overworked and near exhaustion.

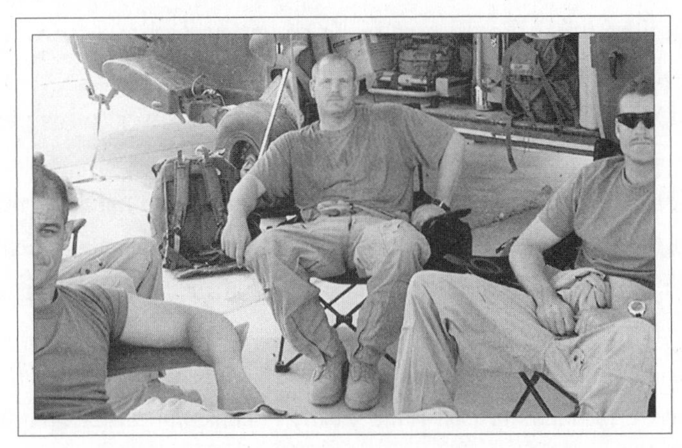

Chris and the crew of Witch Doctor 11 in Iraq

GOLBY FAMILY COLLECTION

"It did not matter how many hours he had in, or how tired he was," Dawn says. Her son wanted to be in the air.

Dawn and Sonya recall that Chris made great efforts to stay in touch with his family.

"He loved me and his kids dearly. He looked forward to spending as much time as he could with his family. He wasn't able to do it too much due to his job. But he did what he could with what time he did have," Sonya says.

When he couldn't see his family in person, he corresponded with them. Naturally gifted with computers and electronics, Chris primarily wrote e-mails out of Iraq. In a couple of them, Chris complained to his mother about the food situation. The chow lines were sometimes as far as three miles away. It would take him so long to walk there, he would barely have time to eat before he was due back in camp.

Dawn took charge. She sent him packages filled with his favorite goodies, including cinnamon-sugar Pop Tarts, Kellogg's Sugar Corn Pops, Doritos, cashews, Slim Jims, canned ravioli, tuna, soda, and bottled water. Some of the food she sent, like a bag of M&Ms that partially melted in the 130-degree desert heat, went straight into something Chris and his fellow soldiers called mystery food. There was no telling what would turn up in the mystery bowl from week to week. You had to wait until you took a bite to find out.

On December 17, 2003, Chris handwrote a letter to his parents.

Good morning, there. How are you guys doing today? I am doing okay out here. We seem to be getting the same old stuff even though we finally caught Saddam. Oh well, at least he is out of the picture. The people around here don't seem to mind so much that he is gone, but there are still a few that aren't too happy. Anyway, not much has been going on out here.

Well, the boxes of food made it okay. Thanks for all the tuna and mayo. These pouches are great, makes it much easier to carry and open while out in the "field." If you can, please send some more of the canned

SpaghettiOs and maybe some with the meatballs. Those make for a really gourmet meal when all you are looking at are MREs [Meals Ready to Eat]. LOL. Besides, when we are out, it's sometimes a mile hike in just for some chow.

So, I hear you got a bit of snow back there. Must be nice. Oh well, it rained here again yesterday, and that made for some really nice mud. It's been so long since we had some good quality mud around here, I almost forgot what it was like. LOL, sarcasm is always fun around here. Okay, well I need to get going. They just got in a new Internet cafe here, and that is what I am using. They have Yahoo! Messenger, so if you are on, feel free to turn on the messenger, and we may be able to chat. I am going to try and be on here all different hours of the day, and mostly during actual day hours for you guys there, so we will see. Alright then, I will talk to you guys later. I am safe out here, so try not to worry, okay? Things are rather slow, even out here at the teams. So until later, I love you guys, and talk to you soon.

Your son, Christopher.

His parents got the following e-mail on January 3, 2004—just after the New Year:

Hello there! How are you guys doing? I am okay. Not a whole lot going on out here really. I am still out at one of the teams. We were busy for a few days, but overall, it is pretty relaxed here. I tried to call on New Years Day, but the phones weren't working too well. Everyone was able to hear the person they called, but they could not hear us. So instead of using all of my minutes up, I just waited to call anyone. Then, I tried to get in here yesterday, and they had this place closed due to the helicopter that went down yesterday afternoon. Obviously, it wasn't me, so don't worry about that. We were just about to take off to go and get them actually, but they cancelled us going. Anyway, I just wanted to let you know that things are going okay here. It's actually a bit boring after a while, but boring is safe, so I can't really complain. I only fly maybe once a week or so actually. The rest of the time is spent sleeping, watching movies, or wandering around trying to find something constructive to do. But mostly, just being lazy. Well, I was just told that my time is up on here. I will talk to you guys later. I love you both, and Happy New Years! Christopher.

He also made time to exchange some e-mails with his stepson, Sean. (Sean lived with Sonya, Chris, and Dylon; Sonya's other son Jonathan lived with his father.)

Dear Dad,
Thank you for the letter. I am doing good in math. I solved thirty-one problems in one minute. Today my goal is to solve thirty-two problems in one minute.

I am doing good with my mom. Dylon is doing good today. I taught Dylon his ABC's. I wrote the ABC's on paper and Dylon read them. Dylon only missed one and that letter was Z. My mom is doing very good today. Dylon is doing good in school. I am doing good in school too. If I have a bad day I will talk to a teacher. I am working on being positive at school.

I am going to work harder to get my work done at school. I am doing good in Mrs. McLachlan's room. And I am awesome! And you are awesome too!

I love you and miss you,
Sean

Dear Sean,
Hello! I am doing good. It was a long trip from home to here at work. I did not get your letter until Thursday morning. It is cold over here now. It is colder here than it is in Colorado! But I am doing good anyway.

I miss you and I miss Dylon too. I had a lot of fun with you and

Dylon while I was there on vacation. Thank you for being good and listening to Mom. That is a good thing, and it makes it easier for all of us. I am sure that you like to have good days, and that is the best way to start them.

I hope Mommy is getting you to the teacher that said she would help you with your reading. If not, then you need to remind her that she needs to talk to Mrs. Scanlan for you and get that started, okay? Thank you for writing to me.

Sean, I want to keep doing this as much as we can! It is good to hear from you, and to be able to talk to you. I want you to know that I think about you and Dylon every day that I am here at work. You keep doing good in school and at home for Mommy, okay? I would like that very much.

If you are having a bad day, please talk to someone so that we can help you turn it into a good day. That way, it can become a good day for everyone!

Thank you again, Sean. Daddy has to get back to work now. It was good to hear from you, and I will talk to you later, I promise!!! I love you,

Dylon and Sean in a Blackhawk cockpit
in Ft. Carson, Colorado

GOLBY FAMILY COLLECTION

Sean, and please tell Dylon that I love him too! Also, please tell your teachers thank you for letting you do this at school. It gives me and you a way to talk to each other, and I like that a lot! Good-bye for now. Dad loves you!

On the afternoon of January 8, 2004, Chris was perched on the side of his Black Hawk medevac copter. He was operating the hoist, getting passengers into the aircraft and safely securing them in a seat or litter. Five passengers were on board Witch Doctor 11, along with four crew members—nine total en route to a hospital in Iraq. The passengers were Sergeant, First Class Gregory B. Hicks, of Duff, Tennessee, assigned to Company B, First Battalion, Ninth Cavalry Regiment, First Cavalry Division, based in Fort Hood, Texas; Specialist Nathaniel H. Johnson, of Augusta, Georgia, assigned to Company D (Aviation), Eighty-second Support Battalion, Eighty-second Airborne Division based in Fort Bragg, North Carolina; Chief Warrant Officer Aaron A. Weaver, of Inverness, Florida, assigned to C Troop, First Squadron, Seventeenth Cavalry Regiment, Eighty-second Airborne Division, Fort Bragg, North Carolina; Staff Sergeant Craig Davis, of Opelousas, Louisiana, with the 142nd Corps Support Battalion, Fort Polk, Louisiana; and Sergeant Jeffrey C. Walker, of Havre de Grace, Maryland, assigned to Company C, 782nd Main Support Battalion, 82nd Airborne Division, Fort Bragg, North Carolina.

Chief Warrant Officer Philip A. Johnson Jr., of Mobile, Alabama, was the pilot in charge of the chopper that day. He was accompanied by pilot Chief Warrant Officer Ian D. Manuel, of Jacksonville, Florida, and two medics: Specialist Michael A. Diraimondo, of Simi Valley, California, and Specialist Christopher A. Golby.

There were no survivors.

Back at home, Dawn Golby was uneasy. She had heard the breaking news that a medevac Black Hawk had crashed in Iraq.

"I just knew it was him," Dawn says. "That feeling was there. I just knew."

She came home from work early and called Sonya in Colorado. She didn't recognize the person who answered the phone, but whoever it was, she was sobbing.

"She was crying and kept saying, 'I am so sorry, Mrs. Golby.'" Eventually Sonya got on the line.

"Is it true?" Dawn asked.

"Yes."

Dawn didn't want to believe her. She hung up and then called right back. She remembers, "I must have called her five times."

Somewhere along the line, Sonya realized the army had not yet visited Dawn.

"I wasn't supposed to tell you over the phone," Sonya said. The army casualty officers made her promise not to. They were planning on making the official visit to Chris's parents after the end of the workday.

At 7:00 p.m., Chris's parents, Dawn and Ronald, watched a car pull up to their house. They saw the driver looking at the mailbox with a flashlight. The two men parked, got out of the car, and put their hats on.

"I just lost it," Dawn said. "I knew it was true."

After the two soldiers finished reading the secretary of defense's statement, she asked one last time, "Are you sure?"

"Yes, ma'am, it's true."

To Dawn, their reply was as biting as the icy January air.

A special memorial service was held at Fort Carson for the crew of Witch Doctor 11. Family, friends, and fellow soldiers gathered to-

Specialist Christopher A. Golby

PHOTO BY DAWN GOLBY

gether in a large hangar. At the front, on a wooden stage, were photographs of the four men, four pairs of empty boots, four guns topped with helmets, and four sets of dog tags hanging from trigger guards.

As the ceremony proceeded, the hangar doors slowly opened. The congregation got a clear view of a Black Hawk helicopter parked on the tarmac. Then they heard a radio call across the public-address system.

"Witch Doctor one-three, this is dustoff operations."

"Witch Doctor one-three, we are operational," came the answer.

There were two more exchanges for other helicopters. Each replied that it was operational. Then there was a radio call for Witch Doctor 11.

"Witch Doctor one-one, this is dustoff operations."

No response.

The radio caller made a half-dozen more attempts, each met by silence.

After the last call, four medevac Black Hawks flew over the hangar. One zoomed off, leaving the others in a missing-man formation. The congregation held a respectful silence.

"My husband was a good man," Sonya says. "He told me the day he left, he joined the army to help people and to defend our country and he was proud of it. I know that he wanted to be part of something and he was."

"He was willing to help everyone and anyone. If you had him for a friend, you had him for life," his mother adds.

"I am just really proud of my husband. I want everyone to be. I want them to know what you can lose and we lost him. But he went doing what he loved. So that helps us all even more. We all miss him dearly," Sonya says.

She continues, "Some days I feel like he is going to walk through the door. I don't think that feeling will ever go away. I just wish it could happen."

January 6, 2004.
Just wanted to let you know that if you hear any news on TV today about attacks on bases over here, I am okay. We had an attack on our base today, but only one person was hit, and it was just a small scratch on his face . . . really nothing serious. I will tell you more about it later, but just wanted to let you know that I am safe. It was, and still is, an interesting night here. Anyway, I should get going here. Try not to worry; things aren't as bad as they seem most of the time. I love you guys, and talk to you later!

Christopher.

THE CIVILIAN

I know you saw the pictures of the prison episode with those prisoners and a few bad U.S. soldiers. Believe me, a lot of us are ashamed of them. They don't deserve to wear our colors.

—SERGEANT PATRICK McCAFFREY

Patrick McCaffrey's strong sense of right and wrong was evident early in life.

Once, when he was in middle school, he saw a big kid bullying a smaller kid. Without a moment's hesitation, Patrick stepped between the two, ushering the larger boy outside to settle the dispute. He was considerably smaller than the bully, but in the end, his sense of justice and decency prevailed. David gave Goliath a lesson in humility.

"He would step into the middle to do what was right," his mother says.

The only child of Nadia and Bob McCaffrey, Patrick loved to ask his mother deep, philosophical questions.

"Mom, why don't people get along?"

"Mom, why are some people a lot richer than other people?"

"Mom, why do people have different gods?"

He flexed his inquisitive mind by reading and speaking fluent French with his mother.

After graduating from high school, he attended De Anza College in Cupertino, California, for a year. But the demands of the real world soon became too great for him: he had to drop out of school to work. He found a niche in a small, family-owned car-body repair shop, working on removing dents and dings. With a winning smile, and the best people skills in the business, Patrick soon was promoted to manager.

By the time he hit his thirty-first birthday, he seemed like he had his life well in order. He was earning a good salary. He had bought two new cars and was making mortgage payments on his home with his new wife, Silvia, and two children, Patrick Jr. and Janessa. (His son, the elder of the two, was the product of a previous marriage. Jannesa was his daughter with Silvia.) He was respected and well liked at the shop where he had worked for ten years, and he found great fulfillment in the meet-and-greet aspects of his managerial duties. His infectious smile made it impossible not to like him from the first glance.

Patrick and his baby daughter, Jessica

PHOTO PROVIDED BY NADIA McCAFFREY

Then the World Trade Center towers fell.

The 9/11 news reports hit the Californian hard. He was, as so many of his other fellow Americans were, devastated. And he was struck by the need to do something.

"What can I do?" he asked himself repeatedly. "What can I do?"

He spoke to a National Guard recruiter.

On October 11, 2001, exactly a month after the towers fell, Patrick R. McCaffrey Sr. signed up for a tour in the California National Guard. He eagerly completed his training and faithfully attended the required meetings and monthly weekend sessions.

"He wanted to help people," his mother says. "He thought he would be helping to protect California."

Patrick planned to use the extra money he would earn as a guardsman to pay for his children's college tuition. He wanted Patrick Jr. and Janessa to have the education that he had been forced to forgo.

He never planned on going to Iraq.

Patrick and Janessa

PHOTO PROVIDED BY NADIA McCAFFREY

Patrick's company, the 579th Engineer Battalion, was called into active duty on January 17, 2004, after the fall of Baghdad.

"When he signed up, he didn't realize he was going to be deployed," Nadia says. "He did not want to leave. He had his family. He was close to his children."

But Patrick had too strong a sense of justice to back out then. He told his mother and his wife that he had to keep his word. He could not, and would not, renege on his duty or the obligation that he willingly accepted, even though it meant facing the danger of going to Iraq.

"I have to stand up for it," he said to them.

On March 3, 2004, his unit departed.

Right off the bat, Patrick noticed that the Guard units were not treated the same as the regular army units. For example, to call home, his unit was required to use a particular bank of telephones that charged fifty dollars per long-distance call. But he tried hard not to let his sense of injustice deter him from doing his duty.

Patrick was acting as a combat lifesaver. It was his job to provide first aid on the field and then get the wounded soldier out of harm's way and back to a field hospital for treatment. As it turned out, the heat of the Iraqi desert took as great a toll on the American troops as Iraqi bullets did. One of his routine duties was treating soldiers for heat exhaustion from the 130-degree desert temperatures.

He was deeply disturbed, almost overwhelmed, by the hatred some of the Iraqi people showed toward American and European troops.

"It was more than he could bear," Nadia says. "So he focused on the Iraqi children and his fellow soldiers."

The Abu Ghraib prison scandal that broke in the spring of 2004 appalled Patrick beyond words. The event so offended his deep-seated sense of right and wrong that he started to second-guess his country's right to be in Iraq.

"He was so ashamed by the prisoner-abuse scandal," Nadia says. "He even sent me an e-mail to tell me that not all the soldiers were like that. He said we had no business in Iraq and should not be there."

Tuesday, June 22, 2004, was another hot day in the desert. Patrick was on patrol with his unit near Balad, about eighty-five miles north of Baghdad. It wasn't yet 11:00 a.m., and thermometers were spiking over 125 degrees. Two men had already become dehydrated from the heat, and Patrick had treated them for their heat exhaustion.

Patrick's day brightened momentarily when some Iraqi children handed him flowers. Their gesture brought him deep joy. A snapshot from that moment—the last photo ever taken of Patrick McCaffrey—shows him holding the flowers, a big, happy grin filling his face.

Forty minutes later, he was dead.

He had been driving a Humvee with a fellow California Army National Guardsman, First Lieutenant Andre D. Tyson, Company A, 579th Engineer Battalion. Suddenly, his vehicle was ambushed. The soldiers' vests provided little protection against the storm of bullets from all directions that smashed through the exterior of the Humvee. Others returned fire, but it was too late for Patrick and Lieutenant Tyson. Both men died on the scene.

Patrick's body was returned via commercial airliner to the Sacramento International Airport on June 27, 2004. The news media had gotten wind of the story, and was there to witness the arrival. They captured numerous photos of his flag-draped casket. Free of the restrictions imposed on air force bases, the media quickly disseminated the images.

On the evening before Patrick's full military funeral ceremony, a memorial service was held on July 1, 2004 in Oceanside, California. Hundreds of friends and relatives attended. Afterwards, Nadia spoke to those who had taken part in the memorial.

"I'm looking at you all now and I cannot believe it."

She continued, "The last time I saw Patrick was on Father's Day. Patrick was glowing that day. Watching him was overwhelming. The joy that was radiating from him, his face had an aura."

She spoke of the last photo taken of her son with the Iraqi children and the flowers they had given him.

"He had the same smile on. That was one of the very last pictures. It was taken a very short time before his death," she said. "Patrick was at peace. Patrick was at total peace."

Although Bob and Nadia McCaffrey had been divorced for years, they were reunited that day in celebration of their son's life, and the shared grief of his loss.

The Guardsman with a new friend, outside of Baghdad

PHOTO PROVIDED BY NADIA McCAFFREY

"The best thing about my son was his affinity to drawing people together and making them friends," Bob McCaffrey later told a reporter. "He was a great man."

"If I asked him to spot me a hundred dollars, he'd say, 'Is that all you need?'" Staff Sergeant Romulo Rimando, one of Patrick's school friends, remembered. In one of his last e-mails to Sergeant Rimando, McCaffrey had written the poignant words, "Well bro, I hope you never come here."

To conclude the memorial, Patrick's friends and family stepped outside for a toast. For the adults, there were shots of whiskey (Patrick's favorite drink, in honor of his Irish heritage). The children were given yellow balloons filled with helium, many with messages or tags attached to them in honor of Patrick's service.

The toast was made. The adults threw back their whiskey, and the children released their balloons. The globes ascended into the sky, caught by the gentle California breeze. Slowly, the yellow spots of color faded away.

"That was just beautiful," Nadia recalls.

The next day, Patrick McCaffrey was laid to rest near Oceanside, California.

A grief-stricken Nadia spoke very little to the media that showed up at her son's funeral.

"I want you all to remember that we are here today to honor our son's memory," she said. "This is a time for grief."

That was all she was to say to the press in attendance. A friend of the family later told a reporter that her reticence to speak publicly stemmed from the fact that she had been misquoted in a *Los Angeles Times* article. The paper had reported that she had invited press to witness Patrick's flag-draped coffin being unloaded from the plane that brought him home, a false rumor that quickly spread over the Internet. Nadia says she did no such thing.

Several days later, one of the balloons that had been released at

Patrick's memorial service was recovered nearly twenty-five hundred miles away in Lewisburg, Pennsylvania. The woman who found the balloon, Anna Barrick, took an interest in the information she found on its tag. She researched Patrick's name on the Internet, found his family's information, and contacted Nadia.

Anna then sent an e-mail message to her coworkers, family, and friends:

> *On the Fourth of July, a yellow balloon with a tag (front) "McCaffrey, Patrick R., Sr. Tracy, CA," (back, Bible verse) "Greater love has no one than this, that he lay down his life for his friends. John 15:13" came down in our backyard. Greg found the balloon next to our back door. We initially thought that a local organization had released a bunch of balloons for a Fourth of July celebration with the names of soldiers killed in action. Still, I kept the tag and brought it in to work to research on the Internet. Today, I finally had time to do some investigating. I found an article about a soldier killed in Iraq on June 22. The article indicated that at Patrick McCaffrey's memorial service on July 2 in Oceanside, California, yellow balloons were released by the children.*
>
> *Can you believe that the balloon traveled across the country in two days and ended up in our backyard? I believe that everything happens for a reason. I found Patrick's mother's e-mail address on the Internet and sent her a note. Who knows, maybe he has a history in Pennsylvania, and this was a sign from him to his family?! Not knowing what to do with this incident, I thought the least I could do was relay Patrick McCaffrey's story.*
>
> *Remember all of those that have fought for our country today and in the past. Whether you agree with war or not, there are people giving their lives for our freedom! Patrick is survived by his parents, a wife, a two-year-old daughter, a nine-year-old son, and countless other friends and family. It is our obligation to remember him (and all of the others)!*
>
> *Thanks for listening.*

Patrick McCaffrey was a citizen soldier who was moved by the events of September 11, 2001, to do what he felt was right. Though some might say he was naïve to think that he would not be deployed, in the face of his surprise, he did not shirk his duty or his responsibility. And later, when he had doubts about what his country was doing, he honored his commitment by staying the course. In so doing, he brought credit to himself, his family, and his nation.

Dear Mom,

Thanks for writing me. It is truly easier to write you through e-mail than through letters. I love the precious picture of my princess. Thank you for that. I am doing ok. I hurt my knee a little, but I'm sure I will be ok. I have been using the medicine cards every day.

Sometimes it makes me laugh as the day unfolds. I know you saw the pictures of the prison episode with those prisoners and a few bad U.S. soldiers. Believe me, a lot of us are ashamed of them. They don't deserve to wear our colors. They will go to prison for a long, long time. Because of what they did, it has become very hard for us to deal with a lot of the Iraqis. But you and everyone else have to remember that we are constantly under attack by these people. They truly hate us. We know not all of them, but you can see it in their eyes as we pass through small villages and towns and cities. I love the little kids, though. They remind me of my own, and I always give them food and water, even though we are not supposed to. You know, I could use a box of flattened soccer balls with a pump and Frisbees. I could hand them to the children as I pass through the small towns. When we help the kids, they tell us where the bad guys are. Just so you understand how bad these guys are that killed that American hostage the other day, they have placed a $10,000 bounty on all American soldiers. So, we stand ready to fight every minute. I gave up my M-16 rifle. I now have a big machine gun that is much more powerful.

Don't worry, I know God is looking out for us and I know it's because of you and Silvia praying for me. Thank you. I would appreciate it if when Silvia comes home, you really try hard to patch things up. That would make me so happy. I know both you and her say that everything is ok, but I want you guys to be as close as before. That makes me so happy, knowing how close you guys are. I know you are having a hard time with me being in constant danger, but I have become very numb to everything and stand very ready. But even though you are having a hard time as a mother, try to imagine how Silvia feels as a wife and mother left behind at home. Please make sure you sit down with her and make each other feel close again, because her feelings are so easily hurt, and then she thinks that you are always mad at her. Remember, she is the opposite of you and holds everything inside and takes everything to heart. I know you know that, but you guys need to become each other's strength. I have sent a box home. It has T-shirts for you, Dad and Silvia, and a teddy bear and hat for Junior and Janessa. I also have a CD in there full of pictures of me and my friends here. It was mostly on our trip from Kuwait to Iraq. Just keep it together with the other CD.

Love, your son,
PATRICK

P.S. I'll try to be home for Janessa's birthday. I have put in for leave for 15 days . . . Love you, Mom.

PURE OF HEART

Every day is starting to feel like the same one, and I guess that makes it easier for me to get by. Right now I am just ready for the "war" to pop off so that we can all get past the worst of this and just wait to go home. This experience is really testing my patience and obedience, and also my character in general.

—*SPECIALIST JAMAAL R. ADDISON*

February 17, 2003, was deployment day for the 507th Maintenance Company out of Fort Bliss, Texas. The soldiers made a final equipment check, posed for family pictures, and kissed and hugged their loved ones good-bye before departing for the Persian Gulf. Jamaal R. Addison, a twenty-two-year-old from Conyers, Georgia, was among them.

Slightly more than a month later, a six-truck convoy from the 507th set out to resupply frontline troops. It was just a few days into the war, but already the army's supply lines were stretching some two hundred miles through Iraq. There was an infantry division miles away that needed support.

Somehow, the six trucks made a wrong turn in the southern Iraq city of Nasiriya. Tired, hungry, and disoriented, the convoy started crossing a bridge. Suddenly, all hell broke loose.

They were ambushed by what was later described as an irregular Iraqi force consisting of two tanks with heavy automatic weapons. The three dozen men and women in the convoy—cooks, welders, drivers, and mechanics sent to provide support to a Patriot Missile battalion—weren't expecting to see combat and were only lightly armed. The soldiers of the 507th, including a woman named Jessica Lynch, were simply outgunned.

The Nasiriya bridge became the site of one of the fiercest firefights in the entire invasion. United States Marines from the First Expeditionary Force arrived and were able to rescue more than half of the trapped 507th soldiers. But the rest weren't so lucky. Later that day, the military's information officers stood at a podium and confirmed that two of the Fort Bliss soldiers were dead and eight were missing. Five members of the 507th had been taken prisoners of war, confirmed by video images Saddam Hussein's regime broadcast across the globe.

The American POW saga continued for weeks. By the time the news broke about the successful rescue of Private, First Class Lynch, the army had determined that eleven soldiers had died in the ambush. One of them was Specialist Jamaal Addison.

Growing up in Conyers, Jamaal loved all things electronic. He was fascinated by Atari games and mastered everything from Pacman to pinball. Later, he would take a keen interest in computers. But Jamaal also loved to read, and it seemed like his young mind had an unquenchable thirst for knowledge. He was an A student in school and consistently made the honor roll.

His two sisters, Celisse and Chanel, always looked to their older brother for advice and guidance—except when he tried to get them

With the family dog

PHOTO PROVIDED BY PATRICIA ROBERTS

to participate in one of his harebrained experiments. Like the time he wanted to see what would happen if they put their arms into a moving drying machine.

"Stick your hand in the dryer," he coaxed.

When they refused, the ever-curious Jamaal put his own leg in. (Of course, it got stuck.)

"He was always taking apart his toys to see how they worked," his mother, Patricia Roberts, recalls. "That was the only trouble he ever got into."

During his years at Lakeside High School in Tucker, Jamaal attended Bible study every Wednesday night at Fountain Memorial AME (African Methodist Episcopal), a small church in nearby Clarkston. Jamaal led others in learning scripture. He often quoted his favorite Psalm verse, 51:10: "Create in me a pure heart, O God, and renew a steadfast spirit within me."

His mother says, "God had a hold on his life."

Jamaal and his sister, Celisse

PHOTO PROVIDED BY PATRICIA ROBERTS

Jamaal graduated from high school in 1998. Although he had participated in the air force JROTC, he only halfheartedly considered joining the military. Instead, he enrolled in DeKalb Technical College and started working several jobs.

Then he heard about the fifty-thousand-dollar education bonus the army was offering its recruits. The straight-A student wasted no time in enlisting. Soon, Jamaal was on his way to Fort Benning, Georgia, for basic training.

After hearing about Jamaal's enlistment, Lieutenant Colonel Sider (one of the JROTC instructors at Lakeside) said Addison had the strength and character needed to be successful in the military. "He was a very nice young man . . . and a very good student," Sider said. "He was good in ROTC. I just wish I had him a little longer."

The soldier life suited Jamaal. Patricia recalls, "He made adjustments. Whatever he was told to do, he would do it."

Jamaal moved to Fort Gordon in Augusta, Georgia, where he studied computers and microwave communication for thirty-two weeks. Then he received deployment orders for Korea. He kept in

Jamaal and his parents, Patricia and Kevin, at his high school grauation in 1998

PHOTO PROVIDED BY PATRICIA ROBERTS

touch with his family during his yearlong tour in Asia, but his mom remembers that he was homesick. He was happy to get back to Fort Bliss, Texas.

With war in Iraq looming, Jamaal took a chance and contacted an old friend from his high school computer classes. He had always had a soft spot for Tek'la. As it turned out, the two still had a lot in common. For one thing, both were single parents (Jamaal had a young daughter named Christian). On January 23, 2003, the two were married. Only a few weeks later, he deployed to Iraq.

"He was reluctant to go," his mother said. "He felt he needed to be here to raise his daughter."

When he did manage to call from Kuwait (where they first were stationed), his mother remembers sensing that he didn't want to get off the phone. To cheer him up, she sent him a box of some of his

The proud father with his newborn daughter, Christian Addison

PHOTO PROVIDED BY PATRICIA ROBERTS

favorite candies, including Laffy Taffy, sour straws, and Atomic Fireballs.

The package was returned unopened.

The Addison family watched in horror as the POW incident unfolded in the news. On Sunday, March 23, 2003, an officer came to their home and told them Jamaal was missing. Two days later, the army confirmed that Jamaal had been killed in action. He was one of the first soldiers to die in the Iraq War.

On May 23, 2003, the Texas legislature passed a resolution honoring the life and service of Jamaal Addison:

RESOLUTION

WHEREAS, Words cannot adequately express the sorrow felt at the loss of Specialist Jamaal R. Addison of Roswell, Georgia, who died in the Iraqi campaign on March 23, 2003, at the age of 22; and

WHEREAS, Specialist Addison, a microwave systems operator maintainer, was one of nine soldiers from the army's 507th Maintenance Company who lost their lives in an ambush in southern Iraq; and

WHEREAS, This courageous soldier graduated in 1998 from Lakeside High School, where he excelled at his studies and was a member of the ROTC; after a semester at DeKalb Technical College and several jobs, he joined the United States Army and completed his basic training at Fort Benning; he received training in communications and spent a year in Korea before being posted to Fort Bliss, from which he was deployed to the Persian Gulf in February 2003; and

WHEREAS, Noted for his seriousness of purpose and ability to get things done, Specialist Addison planned to start his own business after his discharge from the military; his ability to set goals, together with his compassionate and caring nature, also marked him out as a likely community leader; and

WHEREAS, Americans owe an immeasurable debt to their military personnel, whose brave and unfaltering efforts have long secured this nation's treasured freedom; through his unwavering devotion to duty, honor, and his country, Specialist Addison embodied the highest ideals of the United States armed forces, and the State of Texas and the nation now mourn the loss of a hero who made the ultimate sacrifice in his country's behalf, and whose life was a blessing to all who were privileged to share his love and friendship; now, therefore, be it

RESOLVED, That the House of Representatives of the 78th Texas Legislature hereby pay special tribute to the life of Specialist Jamaal R. Addison and that it extend deep sympathy to the members of his family: to his wife, Tek'la Addison; to his son, Jamaal, and his daughter, Christian; to his mother, Patricia Webb; to his father,

Kevin Addison; to his sisters, Celisse and Chanel Addison; and to his other relatives and many friends; and, be it further

RESOLVED, That an official copy of this resolution be prepared for the members of his family and that when the Texas House of Representatives adjourns this day, it do so in memory of Specialist Jamaal R. Addison.

A spiritual man who understood the value of education, Jamaal Addison lived quietly. His last letter home brings to life the tragedy of dreams, aspirations, and a new love being prematurely ended by one wrong turn in the road.

Jamaal Addison's memorial stone at the DeKalb County Veterans Memorial in Brook Run Park, CO

PHOTO PROVIDED BY PATRICIA ROBERTS

13 March 03

Dear Dad,

What's happening, dude? I received your letter not too long ago but I have been unable to write you back until now. Things are starting to pick up speed and very soon things will be going down. Now we are in full battle

gear, and we are also carrying live rounds with us at all times. Probably as you are reading this, things will have already begun. Over these past couple of weeks I have been trying to mentally prepare myself for the situation that lies ahead. I think I have been doing a good job keeping myself busy with work so that I don't get depressed and homesick. It's been almost a month here now and I can't believe that I have endured this long without losing my mind. Every day is starting to feel like the same one and I guess that makes it easier for me to get by. Right now I am just ready for the "war" to pop off so that we can all get past the worst of this and just wait to go home. This experience is really testing my patience and obedience and also my character in general. Being here in Kuwait now is so much more difficult than it was for me in Korea two years ago. Since then my situation has changed dramatically and it has made it more challenging for me, but it is not something that I cannot overcome. I think about you all every day, and I get by knowing that I am getting closer to being with everyone again. By the way, thanks for the news clippings. I appreciate the updates. I don't have access to an American newspaper and I don't watch the news. I get all the information I need firsthand from the people I'm supposed to hear it from. I'm sure that you watch the news to stay informed with the program. That's cool. Just don't get too engulfed into it because much of what they say may not pertain to me or my unit. Once we begin our mission, if I am still able to write you, I will be sure to do so to keep you abreast on my status. There is not much more that I know at this time so I will change the subject a bit. So how are things with you and the rest of the fam? How's your lady doing? I heard from Tek'la that y'all went to the circus and had a good time. I was so glad to hear that. I'm so happy that now, even in my absence, Teke is staying in touch and in fellowship with the family. She knows that she is part of the family and that just because I am gone doesn't mean that she can't be around you all. I really miss her to death and I wait for the day when we can be together again. She is truly and dearly a wonderful young woman and I am so blessed to have her as my wife. I know that she is the one that you have been waiting for me to be with. She's been around for a while but I guess that it wasn't our time until now. I pray that you can find the same in your lady and that things will fall in place. Well, Pop, I gotta go now so that I can get some rest but I hope to hear from you again soon. I love you, Dad, and let everyone else know the same. Take care of yourself.

Love,
Jamaal

P.S. Use the address on this envelope, not the old one anymore.

BLACK HAWKS AND DUM DUMS

I guess we shall let destiny take its path

—CHIEF WARRANT OFFICER BRIAN K. VAN DUSEN

The last thing a wife and mother wants is to be jostled awake out of a deep sleep at four in the morning. But that's a risk you run when you marry a man who gets up at the crack of dawn every day.

Whenever Bridgette would try to go back to sleep, her husband, Brian Van Dusen, would say,

"Get up! You can rest when you die."

"He was always getting us up at the crack of dawn to go do something," she remembers. "Brian was always taking us somewhere. He always had something he wanted us to do."

The Van Dusens would find themselves dressed and loaded in the family vehicle before sunrise, and with Brian behind the wheel, they would soon be off to another full day of outdoor adventure.

Brian was an avid outdoorsman who loved to fish and hunt deer and pheasant. His appreciation for the wild sparked an interest in taxidermy, and soon there were trophies mounted throughout his home.

He was the happiest, though, when he could combine his love of nature with the love of his family. He took his wife and kids on weekend camping trips that included hiking, fishing, and camping under the stars in a tent.

Not even a change in the seasons could deter him.

"He had us up at four o'clock in the morning on winter weekends," Bridgette says. If there was snow on the slopes, Brian wanted his family to be skiing. "He never wanted to allow a day to pass without feeling like he'd accomplished something. He just wanted to go, go, go."

As he said so often, you can rest when you're dead.

Brian had joined the army on a whim. He was on a hunting trip with his family when an army helicopter flew overhead. The young Van Dusen made a snap decision: he vowed to join the military so he too could be a chopper pilot.

The Ohio native was only in his early twenties when he enlisted in a National Guard unit based in Wisconsin. Soon he realized that he wanted more: he decided to go active with the army in order to get closer to his ultimate dream of flying helicopters. He was trained as a systems weapons repair specialist working on Apache aircrafts. Although he didn't yet have clearance to fly the copters he worked on, he was slowly but surely getting closer to his ultimate goal.

It would be several years before Brian finally made it to Fort Rucker, Alabama, for flight training school, where he would be trained as a helicopter pilot. (Fort Rucker had been the center of army aviation training since 1973 and coordinated everything from basic flight training to advanced aviation safety courses.) After a year's worth of training, Van Dusen graduated with the qualifications to fly army Black Hawk helicopters. He became a part of an air assault unit, flying copters designed to blanket enemy positions with a huge amount of firepower when called upon by a field commander. Brian was good at what he did: he was a good pilot and an accurate shooter. And he truly loved his job. He was finally living the dream that had formed years before.

Brian in his flight gear in April 2003

PHOTO PROVIDED BY BRIDGETTE VAN DUSEN

Several years later, Brian found himself stationed at Fort Riley, Kansas. At that point, he had been married and divorced, and was the father of two children: eleven-year-old Joshua and nine-year-old Kelly. He was splitting his time evenly between his work and his kids.

But then a friend introduced him to Bridgette. And life changed forever.

"It was not what I expected," Bridgette admits. At the time, she was a premedical student in college. But she continues, "I knew he was the one."

Brian charmed her with his enthusiasm and heart. He made no attempt to disguise the fast-paced lifestyle Bridgette would have to en-

Brian with his son, Josh, and daughter, Kelly, in 1988

PHOTO PROVIDED BY BRIDGETTE VAN DUSEN

dure if she were to make a life with him. Even before they were married, Brian started getting everyone up early for family jaunts with his two children.

But Bridgette was changing Brian too. She was constantly talking about medicine and saving lives. Soon Brian was imagining flying helicopter ambulances, and delivering people to a hospital where Bridgette would be working.

Brian decided to trade his attack copter in for one that transported the wounded. He started flying a Black Hawk UH-60Q medevac, a helicopter equipped with the capacity to carry six patients on litters, an onboard oxygen generator, and a medical suction system. It offered outstanding patient care: increased survivability rates, longer flying range, greater speed, and added mission's capability. Although the UH-60 was capable of handling adverse terrain and weather, it didn't carry any weapons (except the sidearm each pilot and crew member carried). It had a Red Cross symbol emblazoned on its side to protect it from enemy fire.

The next few years of Brian's life were busy. He and Bridgette married and soon had two children, a daughter, Angel, and a son, Joseph. As a chief warrant officer flying the army's workhorse helicopter used for medical evacuations, Brian had to work twenty-four-hour shifts.

"It was the only thing he didn't like about his job," Bridgette says.

A devoted father, Brian spent every moment of his time off with his kids and wife. His rigorous work schedule prohibited him from taking his family on the much-beloved camping weekends. Even so, he never once spoke of leaving the army.

Following Christmas 2002, Brian was sent to Fort Bliss, Texas, for a couple of weeks. While he was there, he got a phone call saying that another unit was coming to take over his unit's duties. That could only mean one thing: Brian's unit, the 571st Air Ambulance Medical Company out of Fort Carson, Colorado (where the Van Dusens were living), was heading to Iraq.

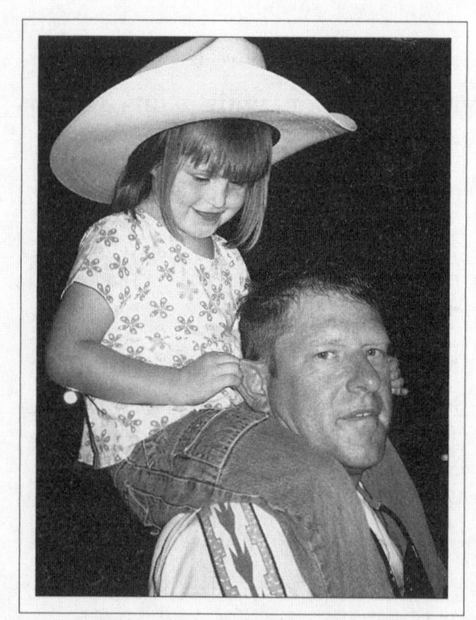

The proud father with his daughter, Angel, at the Colorado State Fair in September 2000

PHOTO PROVIDED BY BRIDGETTE VAN DUSEN

Brian had a ready escape route: he had already been selected to attend an advanced training course. But he voluntarily deferred the post in Germany, which would have allowed him to attend a safety officer school in May. He felt that he had a special ability to contribute to his unit and their new mission due to a previous experience flying a helicopter in Iraq.

After Operation Desert Storm had ended in 1991, the entire Kurdish population of Iraq fled north out of fear that Saddam Hussein would attempt to exterminate them. Turkish officials refused to allow the Kurds to cross the border into Turkey. Hundreds of thousands of Kurds found themselves trapped on barren and rocky hillsides, vulnerable to both Hussein's forces and the harsh weather. Without basic necessities, such as clean water, food, and medical supplies, hundreds died each week.

In April of 1991, President George Bush decided to provide relief and protection to the struggling Kurds. He formed a task force, and in less than forty-eight hours, cargo and fighter aircraft were redeployed to bases in southern Turkey, where they began delivering humanitarian supplies. A United State–led coalition force deployed into northern Iraq, constructed resettlement areas, and established a demilitarized zone for the protection of the Kurds. One of the soldiers that served during the so-called Operation Provide Comfort was Chief Warrant Officer Brian K. Van Dusen.

With nineteen years of army experience, Brian Van Dusen knew exactly how to prepare for deployment. He knew all too well what the army's MREs (meals ready to eat) tasted like, so he wanted to make sure to pack plenty of his own goodies.

He and Bridgette went shopping in a Colorado Springs supermarket. He tossed Pringles and canned meats (like tuna and ham), crackers, and other snacks into the cart. Then they walked past the candy aisle. Brian picked up a bag of Dum Dum lollipops.

"I didn't even know you liked them," Bridgette remembers saying.

"I don't," he said. "They're not for me."

"Then what are they for?"

"They are for the Iraqi kids," Brian replied.

On his previous mission to Iraq, he had dropped candy down from his helicopter to Iraqi children below. Brian intended to do the same thing again on this trip.

"The way to the country is through the kids," Brian told his wife.

Bridgette had been separated from Brian several times in the past—such is the life of a military wife—and was accustomed to saying good-bye. She usually kept excellent control over her emotions. But she remembers that, on the night before he left for Iraq, everything was different.

"The night before he deployed, we went to bed early so that we could take him to the hangar for a 5 AM departure to Iraq. He tucked the kids into bed. I turned out all the lights and crawled into bed next to him. With my head on his chest, these unfamiliar, hot tears began streaming down my face. It was only a matter of time before I was crying uncontrollably. No matter how hard I tried to stop, I just couldn't. Brian tightly wrapped his arms around me and said, 'I'll be back.' I responded, 'You can't promise me that and you know it.' We both fell silent, and soon were asleep. His comment was unusual. Brian *never* made promises like that, not even to the kids. He know it was a promise he had no control over."

But on that night, he made it anyway.

At 8:00 p.m. on March 31, 2003, Brian kissed and hugged his kids and wife good-bye. By 4:00 a.m. the next morning, he was on his way to join his division in the Middle East.

The Fourth Infantry Division, the main unit of Task Force Iron Horse, made up of more than thirty-seven thousand troops from ten military installations, had arrived in Kuwait in late March. The Fourth was a heavy-armor division that sent M1A2 Abrams tanks, Bradley fighting vehicles, 155 mm howitzers, antitank and antiarmor AH-64

Apache attack helicopters, and UH-60 Black Hawk transport helicopters into combat operation. About four thousand soldiers with the division's Third Brigade, also based at Fort Carson, Colorado, were part of the deployment.

Mail service was unreliable, but Brian and Bridgette managed to exchange a few letters in the early months of his stay in Iraq. He lamented that he had not yet been able to pass out the Dum Dums to the Iraqi kids, but was hoping to do so soon.

Tragically, he would never get the chance.

On May 9, 2003, an eleven-year-old Iraqi girl stepped on a land mine. A frantic call went out for medevacs. Brian responded.

Chief Warrant Officer Brian K. Van Dusen was the PIC (pilot in charge). Seated beside him was Chief Warrant Officer Han Gukeisen from Lead, South Dakota. Two army medics, Corporal Richard P. Carl, of King Hill, Idaho, and Sergeant James Sides of Wynne, Arkansas, were seated in the rear. Brian nudged the controls of the UH-60 forward, taking the helicopter airborne from an airfield just north of Tikrit.

He flew in tandem with another medevac. The pair of army copters zipped across the darkening sky to the Tigris River near Samarra. It took about twenty minutes to get to the scene, where they found the girl in critical condition.

There was only enough room along the shore of the Tigris for one of the two helicopters to land. The other UH-60 landed to pick up the girl. Brian and his crew circled about 150 feet overhead. It was close to 7:00 p.m.

There was apparently some tracer fire in the area. Brian initiated evasive action, just as he had been trained. He lowered his hovering helicopter, taking it down to a position just above the Tigris.

Suddenly, the crew on the ground noticed Brian's Black Hawk go into a steep descent. They lost sight of it behind some buildings, but then saw a large piece of debris shoot skyward. The crew immediately presumed the worst.

A nearly one-inch-thick steel cable suspended across the Tigris had caused the fatal blow. Used by the Iraqis to transport items across the river, the cable was not marked on any map. It tangled with Brian's Black Hawk, disabling it and sending it crashing into the Tigris.

"I have no reason to believe whatsoever that they even saw that wire," Major William LaChance, the company commander, would later say. He arrived on the scene just thirty minutes after the crash and reported that there were still tracers in view. It was clear that when Brian descended to what he thought was a safer altitude, his only thought was to try to protect his crew and the aircraft.

Rescuers frantically worked to recover the crew of the downed Black Hawk. But three of them had been instantly killed: Pilot in Command Van Dusen, Chief Warrant Officer Gukeisen, and Corporal Carl. Sergeant Sides was critically injured, but was successfully pulled from the river by the crew of the other Black Hawk and a group of Iraqi civilians.

Meanwhile, back in Colorado Springs, Bridgette was enjoying a day off. She had spent the previous weekend working at the hospital as a clinical laboratory scientist. The kids were at day care; she had found time to mail two boxes to Brian. It was a much-needed period of relaxation.

She got a call from Brian's sister, Vicki Van Dusen. Vicki was watching the news from her home in Charlotte.

"Did you hear about the helicopter?" Vicki asked.

"What helicopter?" Bridgette replied.

Vickie then gave her the first sketchy news reports of a Black Hawk crash in the Tigris.

"I never once thought it was Brian," Bridgette says.

Later, after she had picked up the kids from day care and was settled back at the house, Bridgette decided to order a pizza. When the doorbell rang, she went to the door with her money ready.

It wasn't Pizza Hut's delivery boy she found on the stoop.

Two soldiers, paperwork in hand, in full dress uniform, stood at her door.

Bridgette had grown up in a military family. She knew what it meant when two officers appeared on the doorstep of a soldier's wife.

"Are you Bridgette Van Dusen, the wife of Chief Warrant Officer Brian K. Van Dusen?" one asked.

"Don't do this to me!" she said.

He asked her again.

"Ma'am, are you Bridgette Van Dusen, the wife of Chief Warrant Officer Brian K. Van Dusen?"

"Please, don't do this to me."

But she had no choice but to let them in.

When the doorbell rang again a short time later, one of the soldiers paid for the pizza. The younger Van Dusen kids ate as they watched TV, wondering what the two men were saying to their mommy.

"I was just numb," she remembers.

As the two officers and Bridgette spoke, a bewildered six-year-old Angel interrupted.

"Mommy, I heard one of the men say Daddy had died."

The soldiers respectfully left the grieving Bridgette alone with her children.

A memorial service was held one week later on May 16, in Fort Carson, Colorado. The service was not only for Brian, but also for Chief Warrant Officer Gukeisen and Corporal Carl.

"They were caught in an act of selfless service," Lieutenant Colonel Tom Budzyna said.

The congregation honored the three men who died trying to save the life of a little girl. A bagpipe player played "Amazing Grace." Family members (many of whom who had flown or driven from the East Coast), friends and fellow soldiers gathered in a helicopter hangar to remember the members of the 571st Air Ambulance Medical Company.

"He believed in saving lives, not taking them," David Van Dusen said of his brother.

Chaplain James Ellison reminded everyone that "our last act can demonstrate our life's purpose." Indeed, that was the case for Brian Van Dusen.

"When it came to kids, Brian would do anything," Bridgette later told a newspaper reporter from the *Denver Post*. "He would give his life for a kid. And the funny thing is, he did."

After the memorial service and Brian's funeral, letters trickled home to Bridgette. In August 2003, Bridgette received a huge box containing Brian's personal effects. Among them were two letters he

Brian's family: (from left) Joseph, Josh, Bridgette, Angel, and Kelly after Brian's funeral in May, 2003

PHOTO PROVIDED BY BRIDGETTE VAN DUSEN

wrote to his children, and one to his wife. The notes make it clear that children—both his own and those of strangers—were always at the front of his mind.

Dear Joseph,
Hope you're being a good boy for Mommy! Daddy is working hard. I don't know when I'll be home, but remember, I'm thinking of you! Make sure Mommy gives you a bike ride once in a while!

Love you!
Daddy
xoxoxo

Angel,
I hope you're being a good helper for Mommy. I also heard you're not doing your best in school or in Tae Kwon Do! I hope you will continue to work on your next belt. Remember, if you need to go to summer school, that's less time for you to play! ☺

Regardless, Daddy loves you and misses you very much. Daddy is doing fine. I'm looking forward to coming home and riding bikes with you! If I get home soon enough, we can go fishing again in the mountains.

So please be a good girl and do your best for me. I hope you like the pictures I sent you! I should be able to get some more in the near future! I love you and miss you very much! Take care, and I'll see you soon!

Love you!
Daddy
Xoxoxo
xoxo

5 *May* 2003
Hi Love,
Well, it's Monday again, and we just got back from the Cash. I received your letter and the cards! I love you too and miss you very much. The

weather here is getting hotter and I hope we get A/Cs soon. I'm thinking we will be here till September, but we will need to wait and see. I heard they need 2½ medical companies to cover Iraq, and I think we will be one of them. The only good thing is the $820 a month I'm getting paid extra, along with the tax-free [benefit]. I'd much rather let them keep it and come home now. It really sucks knowing I'm missing the whole summer with you and the kids. I guess I'll continue to lose weight and see how small my waist can get. I know I have already lost some weight, but I have a long way to go!

I guess it's time to play spades. I'll write more later!

Love ya!

Brian wrote his last letter home on May 7, 2003. In it, he speaks of his choice to defer his post in Germany and his desire to return there someday. He tells his wife, "I guess we shall let destiny take its path."

As Bridgette now remarks, "Destiny can be cruel, sometimes."

But her final thought after reading the letter?

"Well . . . now you can rest."

7 May 2003

Good day,

It's Wednesday here again, and so far I don't think we will fly unless we get a mission. The wind is really blowing and testing my patience. I love you and miss you very much!

No word on anything now to tell you about besides the same old bullshit. Miss you all as usual. I was thinking . . . I think we shall still go to Germany when it does come time for us to P.C.S. [permanent change of station]. I don't know how longer after I get back that I will be able to stay in Carson. I'd really like to go back, especially with you! I guess we shall let destiny take its path. Right now the sound of a good German meal with a smooth Pills [Pilsner] sounds awesome. Hopefully I will get a chance to call you again soon. The lines are really long here, so I shall try you from the Cash. Hopefully this weekend. Not that there's too much to talk about. I know you and the kids are doing as well as you all can. Hopefully I'll be home by Halloween.

Love ya!

Me

Xoxoxo

Xoxoxo

THE QUIET KID

I hope to be home soon, but until then I will be out here in this sandy paradise soaking up the rays and sipping on some margarita's. I will write you again soon.

—SPECIALIST DONALD OAKS

In 1991, images of the Persian Gulf War continually streamed into American homes. It was a new kind of interactive war, one that people at home could see unfolding, live, on their television screens.

One of the people watching was eight-year-old Donald Samuel Oaks Jr. from Harbor Creek, Pennsylvania. An intelligent child, Don soaked up the news of the war like a sponge. He was fascinated by the images of the army, their tanks and equipment, and the men wearing desert camouflage outfits. He was captivated by the real-life action depicted in each news account.

Lying on the floor in front of the television, he rolled over and announced, "I want to be a soldier when I grow up."

Donny as a child at home in Harbor Creek, Pennsylvania

PHOTO PROVIDED BY LAURIE OAKS

Don was a typical little boy. He had a collection of G.I. Joe soldiers. He loved Little League baseball, fishing, deer hunting, trips to nearby Lake Erie and the beach, and amusement park rides. He was also an avid collector of sports cards, especially baseball and football. (His favorite team was the Pittsburgh Steelers.)

There were a couple of qualities, though, that set him apart from his peers. One was his uncanny skill with video games. He was unbeatable. His hand-eye coordination quickly became legendary around town. The other was the fact that "Donny O," as he was called, loved to laugh and even at an early age seemed to have the ability to find humor in other people's bad jokes.

"Don was a good child," his mother Laurie says. "He was a model son and a joy to be around. He would do anything you asked." He even agreed to watch after his younger sister, Amber, every now and then.

Although Laurie and Donny's father, Donald Oaks Sr., had

"Donny O's" Little League photo
PHOTO PROVIDED BY LAURIE OAKS

divorced, he was close to his dad. Fishing was their common bond. The two Dons would often spend their time together on Lake Erie fishing for walleye.

With his shining blue eyes and brown hair, Donny was growing into the quintessential image of an all-American boy.

As high school drew to a close, Laurie began pushing Don to start making decisions about what he was going to do with his life. They visited a couple of college campuses, but according to Laurie, "nothing sparked his interest."

It was Paul Witt, a high school friend, who paved the way for Donny O's entrance into the army by joining first.

"We were best friends," Paul said. "We went everywhere together and hung out."

Following Paul's lead, Donny O started talking to an army recruiter. From the start, a condition of his enlistment was that he would be stationed at Fort Hood, Texas. The reason was simple: he wanted to be at the same duty post as Paul. The army agreed and put the condition into his enlistment contract.

Donny O accompanied the recruiter to Pittsburgh for a physical. He also took an aptitude test and scored so well that the army said he could have any job he wanted that was available. It seemed like Don was a natural for the service.

"He was a quiet kid, but pretty inquisitive," Eric Marshall would later tell a reporter. (Marshall was Donny's social studies teacher in both seventh grade and high school.) A retired navy captain, he was known for "spicing up" his classes with stories of the places he'd been and recalled that Don always liked hearing about them.

On March 17, 2000, Don agreed to a delayed entry program with a guarantee of service at Fort Hood. His contract gave him a little time off after his high school graduation in June. He spent the eight weeks preparing, physically and mentally, for basic training. Then, on August 1, 2000, he boarded a Greyhound bus bound for Fort Knox, Kentucky. His life as a soldier had officially begun.

Donny quickly started to show the qualities of a natural-born leader. If another member of his platoon was having trouble, he would help him out, providing enough encouragement to get him through the exercise. He also managed to keep in contact with friends and family from home. Eric Marshall (his social studies teacher) recalls writing him a letter one time and putting "Capt. Eric Marshall" on the return address. (Which, of course, earned Donny some friendly razzing at boot camp for getting a letter from an officer.) Donny also kept in contact with his parents, sister, and grandparents.

As the thirteen-week basic training course drew to a close, Donny started thinking about the next step in his military career. At first, he expressed interest in a job in the medical field, but the army didn't have any positions open. Then the recruiter reeled off the names of several other positions. There was one that really caught Donny's attention: multiple launch rocket systems operator. (Perhaps the name brought back memories of his old video-gaming days.) He decided he should have been off to Fort Hood for AIT (advanced individual training). But a serious problem arose: there weren't any openings in Texas, where he was contractually guaranteed a position.

Chagrined, the army offered to send him to Fort Sill, Oklahoma. They offered him duty stations in exotic locations like Japan or Hawaii. They even went as far as to offer him an honorable discharge. But Don turned all the offers down.

"I don't want to get out of the army," he told them. He just wouldn't settle for anything less than Fort Hood.

It wasn't until after Christmas of 2002 that a spot finally opened up. At long last, Donny was on his way to Texas to meet up with his best friend Paul. When he did get there, the two immediately started making the most of the Texas lifestyle. They often made trips to nearby Austin—two handsome soldiers ducking into malls and clubs. Donny learned to love the big city and everything it had to offer.

But on September 11, 2001, the bubble burst: America was attacked by terrorists.

As soon as he got the news, Donny was ready to go stand up for his country.

"He kept saying, 'I wish I was going,'" Paul remembers.

"I don't want to sit around," Don would tell Paul as they watched other soldiers from Fort Hood be dispatched. "I want to go so bad."

He found contentment, though, serving his country stateside. And even though they didn't at first send him to Afghanistan, the army made it clear that they considered Donny to be a model soldier. He kept being chosen for special assignments.

One time, a commander selected Don to serve as a flag bearer in a general's promotion ceremony (where extra stars would be added to his uniform). Private, First Class Donald S. Oaks Jr. stood at attention in his dress greens, proudly holding the flag. Following the ceremony, he was invited to attend a private reception.

He called his mom to give her the good news.

"Mom!" he excitedly spoke into the telephone, "I got to go to the private reception with the top brass!"

Don didn't let the attention go to his head, though.

"He was a really unselfish person," Paul recalls. "He would offer any help that you needed. He was always giving a helping hand."

One example of the giving spirit was what Donny did on Christmas Eve of 2001. At his barracks, there was a twenty-four-hour-a-day watch and soldiers took turns standing guard. (The army calls it CQ, or captain's quarters.) On Christmas Eve, the soldier that was assigned to the CQ, who lived on base with his wife and children, lamented the fact that he wouldn't be able to spend the special evening at home. Don volunteered to take his post and sent the happy soldier back to his loved ones.

Donny loved to visit the homes of his fellow Fort Hood buddies. He would challenge dads and kids alike to video game matches. No one could beat him. One wife Catherine Pillow, remembers, "I always enjoyed teasing him and my husband when they would play video games for hours on end that, one day, I was going to have to cut their 'umbilical cord.'"

Even though the distance between Fort Hood and Harbor Creek, Pennsylvania, was close to fifteen hundred miles, Donny kept in close contact with his family. He actually grew closer to his younger sister, Amber. An avid writer, she would send her brother poems and letters. Don took to calling her "his perfect sister."

"She inspired him to write his thoughts down," their mother Laurie says.

In return Don wrote a piece of poetry about his sister and sent it to her:

"The Perfect Sister"

Your spirit so happy, your heart so warm—
The words you speak could quiet any storm—
Your personality so gentle, your mind so strong—

With his sister, Amber Oaks

PHOTO PROVIDED BY LAURIE OAKS

You make everything seem right in the presence of all that is wrong—
We have built a relationship far exceeding most that will never die—
There's not a soul that can part us, no matter how hard they try—
You're my best friend, my sister and someone who I receive and give advice to—
To me there's no other person in this world more important than you—
When it seems like you have no one to run to, and you feel lost because you think there's no one who will care—
This is where I come into the picture; anything you need I will always be there—
If you laugh, I laugh; if you cry, I cry—
If I could take back all the pain you've endured for this, I would die—
Even though you're not perfect like we all strive to be—
You're my sister and no matter what anyone says, you're quite perfect to me.

He was able to make some trips back to his hometown. When he did, he always made a point of stopping at his alma mater, Harbor Creek High School, to catch up with his former teachers. The dashing uniformed soldier always took time to talk to students about the army.

As tensions in Iraq heated up in the late months of 2002, Don headed to Fort Sill in Oklahoma for additional training. His desire to do his part in the looming war prompted him to volunteer for the elite "Phantom Thunder" Thirteenth Field Artillery Regiment. There he would be able to take full advantage of his legendary sharpshooting and hand-eye coordination.

He managed to squeeze in a visit home for Christmas. But when he returned to Fort Sill in January of 2002, he realized big changes were in store for him.

Twenty days after he got back to the base, he spoke to his mother on the phone. He was in a somber mood.

"He was apprehensive," Laurie says. She recalls long pauses and silent times during the conversation. He couldn't tell his mother much about what was happening. All he could say was that he had packed his bags.

Then, suddenly, he was gone.

No one heard from Donny O for days.

Her nerves frayed, Laurie finally received a telephone call from her twenty-year-old son, stationed in Kuwait. But he was under orders and couldn't tell her much about what he was doing. His words were guarded. He said he was training and complained a little about the desert heat. But he couldn't give her any details. He only promised her that he would be okay.

Donny also managed to call his father. He confided to him that he would never take life at home for granted again.

"All I want to do is come home, take a shower, be with my family, and go fishing," his father, Donald Sr., would later tell reporters his son said during that conversation.

It was clear that Donny missed his family and friends. Whenever he would call, "he would ask about friends back home, and what was going on," his mother says. "He was often quiet and somber, and kind of distant."

Iraq was one situation Donny Oaks couldn't seem to find any humor in.

For Laurie, April 2, 2003, started like any other workday. She had put in time at her restaurant and run some errands. But when she returned home, there were two telephone messages for her. The army had called, and so had her daughter Amber. A chill went through her when she learned that when Amber telephoned, she was crying hysterically.

"It didn't sound good," Laurie says.

As it turned out, it was Amber, not the army's notification department, that broke the news of Don's death to her. (The notification soldiers had difficulty tracking Laurie down. In their attempts to find her, they somehow found out where Amber was working, and contacted her first.)

Laurie knew that she was supposed to be notified in person in the event of her son's death. But at that point, it really didn't matter. "There is no best way to be notified," she says. When an army officer later informed her that the notification personnel would be subject to disciplinary action, Laurie requested that they let the incident go. Still a mother, she didn't want another soldier to be punished.

Initially, reports of the circumstances surrounding Don's death were sketchy and confused. But soon, details started to emerge. It was late on the night of April 3 when a navy F-15 fighter circling overhead got an order to attack a defensive ring of trucks along the road to Baghdad. What the pilot didn't know was that there were American troops and vehicles in the area.

The "Phantom Thunder" commanders realized the mistake and desperately tried to radio the jet to abort the attack. But it was too late. The plane had launched a missile into the Third Battalion circle. It directly hit the Bradley fighting vehicle occupied by Don and two other soldiers.

On that confused dark night in the dusty Iraqi desert, Specialist Donald S. Oaks Jr., twenty; Sergeant, First Class Randall S. Rehn, thirty-six, from Longmont, Colorado; and Sergeant Todd J. Robbins, thirty-three, from Pentwater, Michigan, were killed by friendly fire. They had all been a part of the army's C Battery, Third Battalion, Thirteenth Field Artillery Regiment (multiple launch rocket system), out of Fort Sill, Oklahoma.

The incident made for a feeding frenzy in the news media. The families of the three dead soldiers had plenty of questions, but had gotten few answers. The Pentagon promised a full investigation.

When Don's body arrived back in Pennsylvania, the city of Erie held his funeral, complete with full military honors, in the downtown Warner Theatre. The town firefighters lined the entrance. They stood at full attention until his flag-draped coffin passed by; then they saluted the fallen soldier. Three Harbor Creek High choirs sang during the ceremony, which was followed by burial in Wintergreen Gorge Cemetery. There, his schoolteacher, Eric Marshall, played the bagpipes.

Back at the Harbor Creek High School, there were over sixty names scrawled across the bulletin board outside the principal's office. Each name was a former Harbor Creek student serving in the military. Donny Oaks took his place at the top of the board, with a gold star next to his name.

A year passed. Finally, the army's investigation was complete. Representatives traveled to Erie to meet with Don's family and presented them a notebook filled with reports. They offered a detailed, three-hour dissertation about the circumstances that took Don's life.

But Laurie took little solace in it. "It really didn't matter," she says. "It's a shame when something like this happens, but either way, friendly or enemy fire, it doesn't change anything."

In the end, it would not have made it any easier for her if her son had been killed by the enemy.

There's no telling what Don would have done if he had returned home safely from Iraq. Many of his friends and family think he would have reenlisted rather than leave the army.

"I am convinced he was a lifer," his friend Paul said.

Whatever he would have decided—an army career or a return to civilian life—Donny O was a patriotic American, a proud soldier, and a devoted son and brother. He left the benefits from his GI insurance to his sister, Amber, so she could finish her studies.

His last letter home is a testament to the love he felt for his "perfect sister."

> *Amber,*
>
> *How are you doing? I'm doing fine. There isn't too much going on out here right now. We are leaving on the 24th and moving farther north. CNN camera crews were with us for three days while we were training. Mom thinks she saw me on one of them. I don't remember anyone taking a picture of me, but they could have without me knowing. How are you and Josh doing? Are you hanging out with Char at all? Have you been saving for a car? How is your job going? Have you been hanging out with any of your friends lately? Tell everyone I said hi. I can't wait to come*

home. Being out here is like being on a never-ending camping trip, but there ain't any trees, just sand and more sand and then after that they got some more sand. They also have bad sandstorms out here at least once a week. It's so bad the day after every sandstorm my throat is raw, my sinuses are clogged up, and it's hard to breathe. I take decongestant pills to break up the sand that is clogging my lungs. The sandstorms are no joke. Besides, all that sand gets all through your clothes, your sleeping bag, and all your gear. You can't get away from it. You have to clean your weapon and equipment every day so that it will work. I would call, but it's been really hard lately because all the phone lines are down, but every once in a while I find a phone to use.

I hope to be home soon, but until then, I will be out here in this sandy paradise soaking up the rays and sipping on some margaritas. I will write you again soon. I'm gonna close for now. Write back if you can.

Love,

Your Brother, Don

The Prankster

Thank you for enduring this time of separation in our lives. I guess when this first started, I did not fully grasp or understand that it was not me, but both of us that were and are bearing the burden of this war. I'm sorry for not understanding this sooner. I know that your sacrifice is greater than mine. I simply changed my uniform, and arena. You sent me off to the unknown.

—STAFF SERGEANT STEPHEN G. MARTIN

Officer Stephen Martin loved to play practical jokes. His fellow police officers at the Rhinelander, Wisconsin, Police Department knew that fact all too well: they were often on the receiving end of one of his pranks. Of course, Officer Martin always made a point of being nearby to see the reactions of his unwitting victims. A well-executed joke would always bring out the prankster's characteristic chuckle.

He was a man who loved to laugh.

"And he loved his job," his wife Kathy Martin says. "He knew he was helping the community, and making a positive change." And in his own way, he was.

Steve and his wife, Kathy

MARTIN FAMILY COLLECTION

Steve moved west to Wisconsin and joined the Rhinelander Police Department in 1996. He had previously been a member of the Trenton Police Department in New Jersey and had also served a tour of duty in South Korea as part of the United States Army's military police.

Wisconsin was a perfect fit for Officer Martin, who was an avid outdoorsman. He liked to go hiking, biking, and deer hunting. On his days off, he and Kathy could often be found in the woods, exploring hiking trails through the immense greenery and rugged terrain of northern Wisconsin. During the winter, snowshoes made the hikes just as enjoyable. Steve loved tramping through blankets of heavy Wisconsin snow.

Love of hiking notwithstanding, it was Steve's riding, not his walking, that made him famous in that small Wisconsin town. He was one of the Rhinelander Police Department's bicycle cops. Patrolling the downtown area on a bike suited him. It gave him plenty of contact with business owners, residents, and, most importantly, kids.

Maybe it was his natural playfulness—the same part of him that enjoyed practical jokes—that drew him to children. Maybe it was just his overall love of life. Whatever the reason, Steve loved being around them. He organized youth bike rodeos. On Saturdays, he taught kids bicycle safety, including the rules of the road, proper riding techniques, and the use of safety equipment.

Stephen Martin had a favorite saying: "Ride hard, shoot straight, and speak the truth." He did just that. He knew when to be serious, and when it was okay to smile or laugh. He had an uncanny ability to adjust to any situation.

Any situation except for one: the period following the terrorist attacks of September 11, 2001. After that terrible day, restlessness took the place of Officer Martin's trademark jokes and bike lessons.

"He felt like he had to do something," Kathy says.

Steve had always regretted leaving the army when he did. His tour of duty had expired well before Operation Desert Storm. He had served honorably, completing a commitment that included a duty

Steve with one of his bike students

MARTIN FAMILY COLLECTION

assignment in Korea. He had made the decision to hang up his soldier's uniform, exchanging it for a police officer's suit. But although he never felt disappointed with his life as a cop, he always lamented the fact that he was not a part of the army when they were called upon to free Kuwait. Now all of those old regrets were returning tenfold, fueled by the fresh wound of September 11.

Steve decided to join the army reserves. On specific weekends, he would take off his Rhinelander Police Department uniform and don the army fatigues as part of the Sheboygan, Wisconsin–based Army Reserve 330th Military Police Detachment.

Luckily, his new military job was perfectly suited for him: he trained other soldiers to be good cops. He taught them how to do their job with fairness and authority, impartiality and alertness, and, of course, good humor. He turned out to be such a natural leader that the army soon gave him the rank of staff sergeant.

Then, word came in December 2003 that the 330th was being activated and sent to Iraq.

Officer Stephen Martin

MARTIN FAMILY COLLECTION

Before Steve left, Harry Whidden, a non-sworn member of the Rhinelander Police Department, presented him with a knife that he carried throughout his two tours of duty in Vietnam. Whidden's relatives had carried the same knife through World War II and Korea.

"Thank you from one warrior to another," Officer Martin said to Whidden as he accepted the token. The mischievous gleam in Steve's eye had become the determined stare of a man committed to serving his country.

Soon Staff Sergeant Stephen Martin was at work in the Iraqi city of Mosul. He was well suited to the many tasks at hand. The city needed its own police force: Sergeant Martin and the other men of the 330th provided the training needed to turn Iraqi recruits into a force that would be able to maintain order in the chaotic country. They were responsible for training over two hundred civilians, teaching them how to use weapons, how to handle proper police procedures and tactics, fire training, and emergency medical care. Another 350 recruits were expected in the weeks to come.

It was a dangerous job: police recruits were highly prized targets for Iraqi insurgents bent on destabilizing the country. In his letters home, Sergeant Martin spoke of the dangers he faced escorting recruits to the training academy. But he managed to stay safe, at least for the time being.

Even in the face of such adversity, Steve didn't forget his devotion to children. He often wrote home to Kathy, asking her to send bags of hard candy. He then handed the candy out to Iraqi children, who would say, "Thank you," in the best English they could muster. Reaching out to kids was, in his mind, part of his mission.

"He said that he was glad to be there because he was giving hope to the next generation of Iraqi children," Susan Fenker, Steve's sister, later explained to an Associated Press reporter.

Along with the candy, Kathy sent anything that she could find that had raspberries in it.

"Raspberry was his favorite," Kathy recalls. So besides the bags of candy, Kathy packed raspberry granola, raspberry trail mix, and raspberry breakfast bars.

Staff Sergeant Stephen G. Martin

MARTIN FAMILY COLLECTION

Despite the many hours Steve spent entertaining Iraqi children (and rereading his favorite book, *For Whom the Bell Tolls*), he always found time for his men.

"I could talk to him about anything," Corporal Matthew V. Groppi says. "Sergeant Martin was very strict when he had to be, but I could talk to him about anything."

Steve, in turn, kept in close contact with friends and loved ones back home. He was constantly writing to Kathy to let her know that he was okay. Reassuring his wife was important to him. The fact that he kept in such close contact with friends and family ensured that he quickly got word from the Rhinelander force that he had been promoted: when he returned home, he would be wearing sergeant stripes on his uniform.

Tragically, he wouldn't live to see them.

June 24, 2004, began like any other day at the interim police academy in Mosul. By 9:00 a.m., most of the crew had parked their vehicles and gone inside for breakfast. A computer had been set up to issue identification cards for Iraqi civilians, but other than that, it was a slow morning. Sergeant Timothy Krolow, fellow Wisconsin native Sergeant Charles "Chuck" Kiser, and an Iraqi interpreter were in the building, along with hundreds of Iraqi civilians.

Suddenly, the three heard a loud noise outside. They realized that it was a car bomb, and that it had detonated on the west side of the academy building. Sergeant Kiser told Sergeant Krolow to continue working on the ID cards, while he, Sergeant Jerry Benzschawel, and Sergeant Martin went to investigate the bomb. But the sound of the explosion had already completely disrupted the academy's routine. Several Iraqi students and instructors had exited their classrooms. Many of the Iraqi civilians waiting to receive an identification card also dispersed.

Corporal Groppi joined the three sergeants as they headed to the roof.

"They got ahead of me because I stopped to put on my OTV [outer tactical vest] and Kevlar," Corporal Groppi explains.

As the corporal worked his way up, he noticed that the parking lot was crammed full of the Iraqis who had formerly been inside.

"When I reached the top of the roof, I looked off to the west. I could not see where the explosion had come from. At the same time, I observed Benzschawel, Kiser, and Martin at the opposite end of the roof," Corporal Groppi says. "I began to make my way towards them. When I was halfway, it appeared as if all three began firing their weapons towards the gate as the sound of gunfire erupted from every direction."

Corporal Groppi carefully worked his way toward the three sergeants.

"When I reached them, I observed numerous individuals firing their weapons below us, and one vehicle approaching the front gate at a high rate of speed."

It was a battered pickup truck loaded with hay, speeding toward the Iraqi civilians and the other soldiers. Sergeant Martin opened fire again, and one of his bullets struck the driver of the truck, who lost control of the vehicle. The speeding truck swerved away from the crowd of Iraqi civilians and the American soldiers. But then it exploded, hurling shrapnel in every direction.

"As I was raising my weapon to fire, the vehicle approaching the gate was detonated," Corporal Groppi reports. "The explosion sent flames past my face, and the shock wave knocked me to the ground. When I got up, it took me a moment to realize I was still alive, not on fire, and had no serious injuries."

In the confusion of the moment, Corporal Groppi grabbed some combat lifesaving bags. As he worked his way toward the sergeants, he found Sergeant Benzschawel, his face covered with blood, a piece of shrapnel lodged in his eye. Corporal Groppi led him down the stairs to safety. He turned the wounded sergeant over to another soldier and then tried to work his way back up the stairs to the rooftop.

As he did, he noticed dozens of seriously injured Iraqis inside the building.

"Most of the injured Iraqis had large cuts all over their bodies. Several were missing large amounts of tissue and flesh," Corporal Groppi recalls.

When he made his way back to the roof, he saw two other soldiers, Sergeant Kristin Thayer and Specialist Michael Rublee, taking cover behind a rooftop water tank. Sergeant Thayer yelled to Corporal Groppi, wanting to know where Sergeants Martin and Kiser were.

"I yelled back that they were at the opposite end of the roof," Corporal Groppi said. Because of the thick, dark smoke, Sergeant Thayer hadn't been able to see them. But together, they managed to make it across the roof to check on Martin and Kiser.

"When I got out there, Specialist Rublee informed me that

Kiser was dead," Corporal Groppi says. Sergeant Martin was critically wounded with a severe head wound and a gaping laceration on his stomach.

Ruplee and Groppi quickly moved Sergeant Martin from the rooftop down the stairs. When they reached the landing, they started emergency first aid. Meanwhile, Sergeant Krolow, who had sustained a head wound in the explosion, had managed to make it out to one of the police vehicles and had radioed for help. He recalls, "I called a medevac, but the helicopter couldn't land. I then tried rounding everyone up to leave, when I heard someone saying that Kiser was dead and Martin was barely alive. I then put Benzschawel and Groppi in a Humvee and told them to stand by, while I ran towards the main interim police academy building. I observed Sergeant Hylman performing first aid on Martin, and then four of us brought Martin down to the first floor. I then heard Thayer yelling about Kiser, that she couldn't carry him, so I had others pull security while I put him over my shoulder,"

Finally, help started arriving. Iraqi ambulances appeared and evacuated the wounded civilians. The Iraqi fire department began to fight the fires; a generator and several vehicles had burst into flame. Over the academy hung a thick cloud of black smoke, dispersed only by several small explosions and sporadic gunfire.

The backup soldiers that arrived were members of a platoon from the 107th Field Artillery Battalion, who were converted to military police in support of Operation Iraqi Freedom. They arrived with three trucks dispatched as part of the Quick Reaction Force. They helped evacuate the wounded and loaded Sergeants Martin and Kiser into Humvees. Meanwhile, soldiers were still providing emergency first aid to the wounded sergeants. Steve seemed to be stable for the moment, but Sergeant Benzschawel was deteriorating rapidly. Corporal Groppi was being treated for shock and head injuries.

Word of the incident didn't arrive in Wisconsin until hours later. It was around 10:00 a.m. when Kathy received a telephone call from Debbie Kiser, Sergeant Chuck Kiser's wife.

"Did you hear the news?" Debbie asked Kathy, her voice quavering.

"No. What happened?"

"Chuck was killed," Debbie said, somehow maintaining her composure. "Steve was hurt too, but not too badly."

Unfortunately, information from the battlefield is seldom 100 percent accurate. It was true that Chuck Kiser had been instantly killed when he was struck by the shrapnel. But the initial report of the severity of Stephen Martin's injuries was inaccurate. Sergeant Martin was in fact gravely wounded and was barely clinging to life.

It took several telephone calls until it became clear just how serious his injuries were.

Medics stabilized Sergeant Martin enough for transport. He was airlifted from Mosul to Germany, and from there to Walter Reed Hospital in Washington, DC, on July 1, 2004. The army made arrangements to fly Kathy to see her husband. But by the time she arrived, the rest of Steve's family had already gathered in the lobby.

"They were just shaking their heads," Kathy remembers. "I lost it."

She recalls thinking that if she could only hold her husband's hand, he would come out of the coma. So she did. But even the touch of his loving wife could not overcome the massive injuries Sergeant Martin sustained while protecting his fellow soldiers and Iraqi civilians. His brain damage was irreversible, and the family made the decision to disconnect life support. Sergeant Martin slipped away.

A single patrol car from the Rhinelander Police Department escorted Steve's body home after it arrived at the Milwaukee airport on June 6, 2004. Gradually, other squad cars joined in, transforming the escort into a procession. Flags in Rhinelander were lowered to half-staff.

Sergeant Martin was laid to rest with the gratitude of the community that he had spent the past eight years protecting. His flag-draped casket lay in state at the Rhinelander High School as a steady stream of police officers, fellow soldiers, and members of the community passed by. Some wiped tears; others made the sign of the cross as they paid their respects.

His father, Reverend Jim Martin, eulogized his son at the ceremony. Reverend Martin said his child was a gift of God who had been returned to his heavenly father.

"It was indeed a privilege to have him," the elder Martin observed.

Following the service (which included Martin's son Seth playing "Tears in Heaven" and "Greater Love" on his dad's guitar), Sergeant Martin cruised Rhinelander one last time. The procession traveled through the streets that he had patrolled so many times on his bicycle and in his patrol car. As the vehicles passed slowly by, their red and blue lights flashing, residents stopped what they were doing to wave American flags. They applauded as the hearse carrying Sergeant Martin's flag-draped coffin passed.

Brigadier General Michael W. Beasley later remarked at a press conference that the congenial Sergeant Martin was "the perfect man for the very difficult job of training Iraqi police officers." He also remarked that Sergeant Martin was a technically proficient soldier who inspired those he taught.

"You can't help but admire someone who stands up and answers the call as he did," added Beasley.

Corporal Groppi calls Sergeant Martin, "a real hero."

"He was truly happy to be there," Corporal Groppi remembers.

Sergeant Martin lived, and died, to serve. In his last letter home, you can feel the grace, warmth, and humor that made him such a beloved husband, father, and soldier.

18 June 04
8:30 p.m.
I love you Kathy.

Hello My Darling,
Today was a very long day. I am not sure why it seemed so long. It was a day off for me. I slept in till 09:00 a.m., and even got a nap in. I did not do anything excluding two meetings, but those were just before dinner. Maybe I just had too much time off today.

I am listening to the classical music CD that you sent me last month. I enjoy listening to it very much. There is so much dirt and filth here, the music helps me go to another time and place in my mind. I know we may never do it, but I like to think about us dancing together all alone in a grand ballroom. Me in a full dress uniform and you in a ball gown. It may sound a little sappy or dreamy, but it is a very soothing dream for me. I miss you with all my heart, Kathy. It is so nice to think about us together, holding each other tight, slowly gliding and turning on the dark marble floor. How I long to hold you close with no one else in the world to talk to us or disturb us. Some days it feels like it will take an eternity for that day to arrive, but I know that the day will come for us. I love you.

The mood and predictions of what will happen on June 30th change every day here. One day, the leadership says nothing will change. The next, everyone acts like the sky is falling. I think some attacks may pick up for a couple days, but calm down just as fast. It just is what it is, nothing more, nothing less. I will deal with whatever comes my way. One thing that I have been made to deal with here is not living by my time table. I may even be able to do something spontaneous when I get home (maybe), but do not hold me to it.

I do not think this deployment has changed me any, other than my growing love for you. This separation has really driven home how much of a part of my being you are. Thank you for enduring this time of separation in our lives. I guess when this first started, I did not fully grasp or understand that it was not me, but both of us that were and are bearing the burden of this war. I'm sorry for not understanding this sooner. I know that your sacrifice is greater than mine. I simply changed my uniform, and arena. You sent me off to the unknown.

I love you, and know that I have never been loved so much as you love me. Thank you, my darling love Kathy.

Your loving & devoted husband,

Stephen

THE MARINE BLUEPRINT

I am proud to be a part of enduring freedom fighting for the American people to abolish terrorism. I can't wait to see you all again.

—LANCE CORPORAL THOMAS J. SLOCUM

If there's one thing the Marine Corps knows how to do, it's how to turn an inexperienced recruit into a razor-sharp warrior. They know how to take a young, troubled kid and mold him into a model American soldier. It's a blueprint, really—a set of plans that has built the most feared fighting force in the world.

But the Marine Corps is more than a collection of highly skilled soldiers. It is a family. It is a kinship as old as the country itself, forged from the blood of countless battles. Together they sweat and toil; together they experience the thrill of victory and the agony of defeat. Together they live, and together they die. That is their way. That is their corps.

Thomas "Tommy" Slocum was born April 20, 1980. He was a restless baby. His mom, Terry Cooper, remembers that he often refused to take a nap during the day.

"Thank goodness for those baby swings," she recalls. Otherwise, "I wouldn't have been able to get a thing done when he was little."

With his angelic blonde hair, little Tommy grew into quite a charmer.

"He got good grades from his teachers," his mom says. "He charmed them into giving him better grades."

But even as a boy, his life was complicated. Terry and Tommy's father, Tom (for whom he was named), divorced, and she became a single mom. Young Tommy felt the responsibility of being the man of the house.

The same little boy that wanted to be strong for his mother, though, still delighted in eating McDonald's Happy Meals and collecting the toys in each box. Terry, Tommy, and his younger sister, Ann, would often have carpet cartoon picnics. Terry would make

Tommy's kindergarden graduation, 1984

PHOTO BY TERRY COOPER

special minisandwiches, and the three of them would settle down on the living-room floor to watch a double feature of cartoons.

Years later, it was his mother who first suggested to Tommy that he consider joining the military when he graduated from high school. She thought it was a good idea for every man to consider serving. But at age fourteen, Tommy flatly rejected the idea. He was testing his boundaries, showing signs of what Terry calls "independent thinking." He had friends and interests in school: he sang in the school choir and participated in gymnastics. His teachers thought highly of him. But he was rebellious, and school didn't provide any kind of true motivation for him.

Then, a few years later, completely out of the blue, it happened. Tommy came home from school and asked his mom if it was okay if he talked to a marine recruiter.

"It floored me," Terry recalls.

The moment Tommy became a marine recruit, his world changed. He still had a year of high school to complete (he was only seventeen years old at the time). But he was already being closely monitored by a gunnery sergeant. And the "gunny" finally managed to squeeze the last few drops of defiance out of him.

One time, Tommy was ordered by his gunnery sergeant to be somewhere after school. On that day, though, the recruit decided to rebel: he didn't show up.

He quickly learned that the United States Marine Corps wouldn't put up with that kind of behavior.

"The gunnery sergeant was here knocking on the door, looking for him," Terry recalls. "As he was getting ready to leave, he saw Tommy walking down the block."

Tommy Slocum was soon facedown, paying for his indiscretion with a seemingly endless set of push-ups—a spectacle that the neighborhood quite enjoyed seeing. If Tommy had been looking for a challenge, he certainly found one in the life of a marine recruit.

Slowly but surely, Tommy's life got on track. During his final year of high school his grades significantly improved. (Graduation was a marine requirement.) His new sense of discipline earned him a spot, for the first time, on his high school honor roll.

Seven days after his high school graduation, Tommy found himself in the middle of Marine Corps recruit training. He was learning the basics of the Corps way, everything from shooting to first aid.

"He called home one time, and he was ecstatic," Terry remembers. "He had just washed one of the marine's tanks. I could never get him to wash my car."

Tommy earned the nickname Cookie Monster at boot camp because he was constantly asking his mom to slip a few extra cookies in his next package from home. But he also proved himself to be a gifted marine, earning the privilege of wearing the corps insignia of the

The Skyview High School graduate, May 1998

PHOTO BY TERRY COOPER

eagle, the globe, and the anchor. The marine motto of "Duty. Service. Honor." was now his own.

In February 2003, Tommy's parents got a letter from his platoon commander. The note made it clear just how well the once-troubled kid was fitting into the Marine Corps.

February 2003

Mr. And Mrs. Cooper,

I wanted to write a quick note and let you know how well your son, Lance Corporal Slocum, is doing since his assignment to our rifle platoon. One of the highlights of my job as a platoon commander is the opportunity to train, mentor, and teach marines during their formative years in the United States Marine Corps. Lance Corporal Slocum has been an outstanding marine who has diligently applied his time and efforts to learning his duties and responsibilities since joining the command. That is no small feat when you consider the stress, changes, requirements, and rigors of military life. Lance Corporal Slocum's perseverance while undergoing

Tom and his mom at the Marine Corps Recruit Day Parent's Night, August 1998

PHOTO BY STAN COOPER

this constant scrutiny by the military chain of command has been outstanding.

I realize that having your son join the military and leave home can be a difficult time for parents. I wanted to personally convey to you how well Lance Corporal Slocum is doing in our platoon. You should be proud of his accomplishments. Lance Corporal Slocum is an excellent marine who I believe will make significant contributions to the Marine Corps and our country. As he progresses and becomes a noncommissioned officer, the marines he will eventually lead will be fortunate to have a leader of such high caliber and abilities. The United States Marine Corps and the nation owe you a debt of gratitude for raising and mentoring an outstanding American.

I thank you for your time, and look forward to meeting you if you visit Camp Lejeune. If I can be of assistance or answer any questions or concerns, please write to me.

Sincerely,
1st Platoon Commander
2nd Lieutenant Swantner
United States Marine Corps

But by that time, the tremendous pride that Tommy, who now went by Tom, took in being a United States marine was already very evident to his family. Tom wore his uniform to the wedding of his mother Terry to Stanley Cooper in 1998.

"It must have been ninety degrees at the wedding," Tom's uncle, Jim Slocum, would later tell a newspaper reporter. "I took off my coat and tie, but you couldn't get him to take his dress blues off."

For a long time, Tom saw Stan as an intruder bent on taking over his position as man of the house. But the marine lifestyle changed his attitude. He started to focus on the common bond that military service formed between him and his new stepfather (Stan had served in the United States Navy). Eventually, the two grew very close.

T.J.'s Marine Corps boot camp graduation photo

PHOTO PROVIDED BY TERRY COOPER

Over the next four years, Tom. got to see the world. His duty assignments took him to exotic locations. He was in Okinawa, Japan, on the day that his official commitment to the corps ended in 2001. And it was in Okinawa that he, without hesitation, raised his right hand and pledged another four years to the marines.

Maybe it was what happened on September 11, 2001, that prompted Tom to reenlist. Maybe it was his sense that he might have a chance to, as he used to say as a boy, "shoot guns and blow things up" that pushed him to renew his oath. Both of those factors certainly contributed to his decision. But the truth was that life outside the corps wasn't really an option for Tom anymore. He had found a family, and a brotherhood, that he believed in.

The marines have always been the United States' primary offensive force—the battering ram, the first troops in, the ones who smash the enemy's front door. Tom was now a part of that prestigious fighting force, and when the orders to deploy to Iraq came, he intended to make his country proud.

The young marine shone even on the transport ship from Camp Lejeune. Because of his previous training, he was able to help prepare his fellow warriors for combat in the desert. He excelled as an instructor and immediately won the respect of the younger marines.

On Sunday, March 23, 2003—the fourth day of the Second Gulf War—Tom and the First Battalion, Second Marine Regiment, Second Marine Expeditionary Brigade, were pushing across the Iraqi desert. The sun had just started to rise in Nasiriya, and for the moment, everything was peaceful and quiet.

Suddenly, all hell broke loose.

Iraqi soldiers, dressed as civilians and carrying white flags, ambushed the approaching marines. The fierce fight that ensued lasted eight hours.

When it was over, twenty-six marines lay dead. One of them was Tom Slocum.

Back in Thornton, Colorado, Terry Cooper could sense that something was wrong. She had been constantly watching the news and had heard reports of major American casualties.

"I knew that day my son had died," Terry says. "I just knew."

The following day, she was at her office in the claims department of her insurance company when the telephone rang. It was her daughter, Ann.

"Mom. There are two uniformed marines here. They want to know where you are."

Terry knew what it meant. Her premonition from the day before was coming true.

"I just lost it," Terry remembers.

It took the two officers forty-five minutes to drive to her office to deliver the official news. When Terry saw the two were wearing their dress blues, "I lost it again."

Tom was the first casualty from Colorado, and his death attracted massive local media attention (especially because of the state's military installations). The young marine's funeral service, which was held on Thursday, April 10, 2002, was packed.

By the time the hearse arrived at the church in Northglenn, Colorado, a large crowd had gathered outside. Many wore uniforms—army, navy, air force, and marine. Sheriff's deputies and firefighters were in attendance. Young children and grandparents—the entire town turned out to honor Tom Slocum. One couple unfolded a huge sign that read, "God Bless You."

Several marines formed an honor guard on the steps of the Immaculate Heart of Mary Catholic Church. They lined up along the church entrance, standing perfectly straight, their white hats aligned, their weapons at order arms.

They snapped to present arms for Tom's casket as it passed by. They did it again for his family as they entered the church. The marines in attendance exemplified the meaning of the marine motto, "Semper fidelis (semper fi)"—"Always faithful." And on the day of his funeral, it was clear that Tom had truly learned the meaning of the phrase too.

Colorado Governor Bill Owens attended the service and said of the Marine, "He reminds us of the profound cost of freedom."

Tom's uncle, Steve Slocum, read a patriotic poem. A few days earlier, he had told a newspaper reporter, "This country was built on people just like him."

Reverend Rod Roberts said, "This is not fair. We shouldn't be here. We should have to deal with him as a cranky old veteran complaining about kids, forgetting he was young once."

But life isn't always fair. And Tom wasn't coming back.

Terry would later realize that many of the nine hundred people who had come to her son's funeral had never met Lance Corporal Thomas Slocum. They were simply there to honor his sacrifice and service.

A shiny black hearse carried the young marine's body to Fort Logan National Cemetery. As it proceeded slowly down the streets, people assembled to show their support and respect. Some held signs; others waved flags. One of the signs said, "We will never forget."

At the cemetery, Tom's father Tom wrote a message on his son's casket.

"Job well done. I love and am very proud of you." According to newspaper reports, he ended the message he inscribed with the phrase he and his son always used to start their conversations, "*Que pasa?*"

"There was so much I needed to tell him that I didn't get to tell him when he was alive," Tom Slocum, Sr., said regretfully.

Air force and army guards stood at attention. The marines fired a twenty-one-gun salute to their fallen comrade. One of the marines played taps. Other marines carefully folded the flag that had covered Tom's casket and presented the flag and the Purple Heart he had earned to his parents.

He would have celebrated his twenty-third birthday ten days later.

For weeks after the funeral, Stan and Terry Cooper received hundreds of letters. Some were simply addressed to "Family of Tommy Slocum, Colorado." (Somehow, the United States Postal Service knew where the letters were supposed to be delivered.) Others were official condolences from military leaders and government officials.

"I looked forward to the mail coming," Terry Cooper recalls. "It helped us when we saw the number of people who were touched by this."

Stan adds that it helped that they did not have to go through the ordeal alone.

Tom and his family

PHOTO BY STAN COOPER

Terry admits that a year after her son's death, she still has trouble coping with the loss. The day that Tommy's regiment returned home was particularly tough for her.

"I fell apart that day," she says. "I could not function."

Sometimes she still seeks solace in her son's small bedroom, decorated with American-flag wallpaper and matching drapes. Terry sits in a chair facing the glass case that holds Tom's Medal of Valor and Purple Heart medal. The same case holds over one thousand letters of support and condolence sent by people she has never met.

"Those cards and letters are what kept me sane," she says. "Hearing from all those people was wonderful."

They donated the thousands of dollars they received to the Navy Marine Corps Relief Society and other military charities.

Thomas Jonathan Slocum was a teenager with a chip on his shoulder, until the marines took him in and turned him into a man. They made him strong, physically and mentally.

"Once he got in the marines," Stan Cooper remembers, he was in it all the way. He didn't do anything halfway."

He was so dedicated to his duty that he rarely found time to write to his parents. And when he did, his letters were brief. But on March 2, 2003, he wrote home on a colorful piece of Marine Corps stationery. His last letter, though short, is filled with purpose and a sense of duty.

In other words, it is the letter of a true marine.

March 2, 2003

Dear Mom and Stan and Annie

Hi. Sorry I didn't write to you guys sooner but I've been busy training, making sure my marines are ready. I'm fine and doing well. I went through the Atlantic Ocean up to the Strait of Gibraltar, into the Mediterranean Sea down through the Suez Canal, into the Red Sea and the Persian Gulf, up through the Arabian Sea, and now I'm in Kuwait. I can't tell you what I'm doing because it's classified, but I'm all right. I hope all of you are doing well. Please keep me updated on everything new. I'm a team leader now and I am getting promoted twenty-nine days from today on April 1. I am proud to be part of enduring freedom fighting for the American people to abolish terrorism. I can't wait to see all of you again.

P.S. Send pictures, and send everyone my love and best wishes.

Sincerely,
Tom Slocum
LCPL US MC
Semper Fi
Orah.

THE CHANCE ROMANCE

You complete me in every way.

—SERGEANT MICHEAL EUGENE DOOLEY

In September of 2000, Christine Garard, a biology student at Pittsburgh's La Roche College, decided to write a letter to a soldier. The suggestion had been her mother's. Christine was lonely at school and wasn't getting much mail. Her mom proposed that she contact someone stationed overseas.

Christine found the Web site for a program called Adopt-a-Platoon and picked the name of a possible pen pal: Micheal Eugene Dooley, a soldier stationed in Bosnia. After a few more weeks of deliberation, she wrote to him. She never really expected to get anything in return.

Micheal Dooley was uncertain about what to do with the note he got in the mail from the girl in Pennsylvania. The only reason he was even in the letter program was because his buddy, Army Medic John Washburn, had convinced him to join. He thought the letter was nice, but felt certain that he wouldn't write back. After all, what could he say to a perfect stranger?

But he remembered what Washburn had said when he told his friends about the program.

"The only thing I asked was that if someone sent a care package or letter, to please write them back and say thank you," John recalls.

So Micheal waited another couple of weeks. And then he wrote.

A surprised Christine quickly wrote a reply to the letter she got. Soon, the two were corresponding regularly through letters and e-mails. Christine heard Micheal's voice for the first time on her twentieth birthday when he called her from Bosnia.

Sergeant Washburn remembers how quickly the romance between the two blossomed.

"While we were deployed to Bosnia, he had the opportunity to take an R & R trip to Budapest, Hungary. When he returned, he ran up to me and said that he had a great time and would tell me about it later, but first he wanted his mail so he could read the letters from his pen pal."

Washburn adds, "I would ask him throughout the deployment if he had heard from his girl lately, and he would get a very big smile on his face and say, 'She has been writing to me a lot, and I am going to meet her after we return to the States.'"

In May of 2001, Micheal returned home to Fort Stewart, Georgia. But he was quickly on the road again. As soon as he got leave, he set off for Pittsburgh to meet the twenty-year-old woman that had captured his imagination and his heart.

Christine remembers exactly how she felt when she first saw Micheal Dooley.

"As soon as I walked through the doors, I saw him and I thought to myself, 'I am going to marry that man,'" she proudly remembers. "I started shaking. He walked over and gave me a hug, and he asked me why I was trembling. But I said I was just nervous."

The Chance Romance

You complete me in every way.

—SERGEANT MICHEAL EUGENE DOOLEY

In September of 2000, Christine Garard, a biology student at Pittsburgh's La Roche College, decided to write a letter to a soldier. The suggestion had been her mother's. Christine was lonely at school and wasn't getting much mail. Her mom proposed that she contact someone stationed overseas.

Christine found the Web site for a program called Adopt-a-Platoon and picked the name of a possible pen pal: Micheal Eugene Dooley, a soldier stationed in Bosnia. After a few more weeks of deliberation, she wrote to him. She never really expected to get anything in return.

Micheal Dooley was uncertain about what to do with the note he got in the mail from the girl in Pennsylvania. The only reason he was even in the letter program was because his buddy, Army Medic John Washburn, had convinced him to join. He thought the letter was nice, but felt certain that he wouldn't write back. After all, what could he say to a perfect stranger?

But he remembered what Washburn had said when he told his friends about the program.

"The only thing I asked was that if someone sent a care package or letter, to please write them back and say thank you," John recalls.

So Micheal waited another couple of weeks. And then he wrote.

A surprised Christine quickly wrote a reply to the letter she got. Soon, the two were corresponding regularly through letters and e-mails. Christine heard Micheal's voice for the first time on her twentieth birthday when he called her from Bosnia.

Sergeant Washburn remembers how quickly the romance between the two blossomed.

"While we were deployed to Bosnia, he had the opportunity to take an R & R trip to Budapest, Hungary. When he returned, he ran up to me and said that he had a great time and would tell me about it later, but first he wanted his mail so he could read the letters from his pen pal."

Washburn adds, "I would ask him throughout the deployment if he had heard from his girl lately, and he would get a very big smile on his face and say, 'She has been writing to me a lot, and I am going to meet her after we return to the States.'"

In May of 2001, Micheal returned home to Fort Stewart, Georgia. But he was quickly on the road again. As soon as he got leave, he set off for Pittsburgh to meet the twenty-year-old woman that had captured his imagination and his heart.

Christine remembers exactly how she felt when she first saw Micheal Dooley.

"As soon as I walked through the doors, I saw him and I thought to myself, 'I am going to marry that man,'" she proudly remembers. "I started shaking. He walked over and gave me a hug, and he asked me why I was trembling. But I said I was just nervous."

Later, Micheal would tell one of his army buddies that when he saw Christine, it was "love at first sight."

The trip to Pittsburgh that was supposed to last only one day turned into a week. The following month, Christine flew south to spend another week with Micheal. Soon they were talking about marriage.

Later that summer, Micheal traveled back to Pittsburgh to ask Christine's father, Bill Garard, for permission to marry his daughter. He promised that he would see to it that Christine finished college and got her degree. And he vowed that when his commitment to the army was over, he and Christine would move to Pennsylvania. Bill consented, and in that moment, the dream that had formed in Christine's heart the moment she first saw Micheal became a reality.

In the early months of 2002, the couple was blissfully happy. They had time to indulge in their mutual passions during their frequent visits to each other. Both animal lovers, Micheal and Christine often visited the zoo. They went on skating adventures, Christine

Micheal and Christine in 2001, right after they got engaged

DOOLEY FAMILY COLLECTION

settled comfortably in her in-line skates, Micheal balanced precariously on his skateboard. The only shadows in their perfect world were the rumors that were flying about deployment to the Middle East.

The couple decided not to wait any longer. Christine interrupted her college studies and moved to Georgia, where she and Micheal married in a civil ceremony in March of 2002. Then Micheal, Christine, their two dogs, and four cats moved to Fort Carson, Colorado, where his unit was based.

From that point on, life sped up for the pair. On February 11, 2003, Christine learned she was pregnant. Micheal ran into Sergeant Washburn, who was also at Fort Carson, a few days after he got the good news. (He didn't know it at the time, but it was to be the two friends' last meeting.)

"He very proudly told me that since we last saw each other at Fort Stewart, he had gotten married to his pen pal from AAP [Adopt-a-Platoon] and that they were expecting a baby in October," he recalls. "As I looked into his eyes, I could see the joy and pride that comes with finding out you're going to be a father. I will never forget just how proud he was of his wife, Christine, but also that he was finally going to be a daddy."

The happy couple in 2002
DOOLEY FAMILY COLLECTION

A mere three days later, Micheal got word that his division, the Third Infantry, was deploying to Iraq.

April 11, 2003, was a difficult day.

Christine woke up early in the morning, crying. "It was horrible," she remembers. "It was just tearing Micheal apart."

Neither of them wanted to say

good-bye. Micheal was ecstatic at the thought of being a father, and the idea of leaving his wife and his unborn child (which an early ultrasound had determined would be a boy) was "ripping at his heart." After he left, Christine cried for three days straight. She was only able to stop when she told herself that she had to pull herself together for the sake of the baby.

Once Micheal arrived in Iraq, the couple developed rituals that helped them stay close despite the distance between them. Usually once each week, Micheal was able to call Christine.

"Every night, I would take my cell phone to bed with me since that's when he would usually call—in the middle of the night," Christine said. "When I went to bed, I would say, 'Good night,' to his picture and kiss it, then blow him a kiss every night at midnight, no matter where I was."

In one very special phone call, Micheal told Christine that he had chosen a name for his son.

"Shea Micheal Dooley," he said, his voice bursting with the pride of a daddy-to-be.

Christine would also send Micheal packages and letters, some as long as sixteen pages.

"In my letters I would tell him what I did on a daily basis, how the pregnancy was going. I always let him know how much I supported him. And I would decorate the letters and the packages with stickers that expressed my love for him. For example, heart stickers that said, 'I love you.' Every time we would write, we always would write, 'I love you,' all over the letters," recalls Christine.

Her packages included Slim Jims, packages of Kool-Aid mix, and disposable cameras. One time, in response to a special request, she sent a baseball mitt and ball. (Baseball had always been Micheal's favorite sport.)

Micheal pored over every letter and parcel his wife sent, treasuring the mementos from home.

"I kiss your picture and the baby's ultrasound picture every day when I wake up and before I go to sleep," Micheal told his wife. Later, members of his platoon would recall that he looked at those two pictures constantly.

The soldier found time to write to his wife too. He always made sure to tell Christine that it was the thought of her and their unborn child that kept him strong.

Hey, Baby,
April 15, 03
How are you doing? I am fine. We are sitting here at the port and downloading our vehicles off of the boat. It has been up in the hundreds out here for the past three days. The base camp we are on has nothing. We have tents to sleep in but the floors are hard as hell. There aren't any phones here so we can only write letters for now. It sucks but we can handle it. I miss you so much but I am strong and will make it. You are strong too and I know you will be okay. You have to be for my baby so he can be healthy when he comes out to see the world. I can't wait till I get home and give you a big hug and kiss. You are the love of my life and I wouldn't change anything about our lives. I don't know what I would do without you, probably go crazy. I don't know what our mission is yet, but I will take care of myself. You know I will.
Love always,
Micheal

With his wife's support from home, Micheal Dooley made the most of his time in Iraq. He was promoted to sergeant, a remarkable achievement for the twenty-three-year-old. He had always been a talented soldier: he joined the army the year after he graduated high school in 1998 and immediately became an outstanding recruit, earning a spot in the Excellence in Armor Program. But getting a promotion at such an early age was a true accomplishment, even for someone as naturally gifted as Micheal. It seemed he was not only surviving, but also flourishing in the hot Iraqi desert.

Then tragedy stuck on Sunday, June 8, 2003. Sergeant Dooley was standing his post at a checkpoint in Al Qaim, located in the northwestern section of Iraq near the Syrian border. Three men approached him, asking for medical assistance for a friend. Then they opened fire from about fifteen feet away. One of their bullets smashed into Micheal's face, just below the left side of his nose. Medics worked to save him, but the ambush had been successful. Micheal succumbed to his wounds even as medics frantically scrambled to save him at a hospital in Al Asad. One of those medics was John Washburn.

He later recalls the horrific details. It was about 11:30 p.m. "I was walking back from our squadron headquarters and heard a helicopter out back of the hospital. I got a very uneasy feeling inside of me," he says. "As I walked into the trauma bay and saw my fellow medics doing CPR on yet another soldier, I heard the doctor call the time of death. I remember hearing the medic that was recording everything ask if anyone knew who the soldier was. All they had was Dool-something."

Sergeant Washburn's attention snapped into focus.

"I walked over to the patient's right side and looked very closely at him. I looked at his right shoulder and saw the tattoo Micheal had gotten in Hungary," he recalls. "I told the recorder that his name was Sergeant Micheal Dooley. My heart dropped to the floor as I stared at his body just lying there."

Sergeant Washburn told the medics he wanted to help because Dooley was a former soldier of his.

He carefully removed all the tubes from his friend's lifeless body and cleaned as much blood off it as he could. He then placed Micheal into the body bag.

"I wanted to escort him as far as I could," Sergeant Washburn remembers.

"Three other people helped me carry his body out the back doors to where we had to meet the truck. As we walked past a small group of soldiers from my unit, everyone came to attention and I could see the tears in their eyes. The truck was not there yet, and the soldiers were given the option to place his body on some stands until it arrived. But we all decided to stand there and hold him until it did."

Back at her parent's house in Murrysville, Pennsylvania, Christine was feeling uneasy.

"I just knew something was wrong," she remembers thinking. Now five months pregnant, she was accustomed to being jolted awake around 3:00 a.m. each Monday morning by Micheal's weekly telephone call. But at 3:30 a.m. on the morning of June 9, she was awake and restless. The phone still hadn't rung. She managed to fall back to sleep by dreaming about when Micheal would be home. They would remodel their deck and build a nursery for their baby.

"I just remember dreaming how it would be," she said.

But around noon, those dreams were permanently shattered. She answered a knock at the door and found a uniformed army officer waiting for her.

"This can't be happening," Christine remembers saying.

"I need to come in and talk to you," the officer told her.

Christine knew right away what he was going to tell her, but at first she refused to accept the news.

"I was trying to find something so I could prove they were wrong, that it was not Micheal."

She demanded to know the middle name of the soldier that had been shot and killed. She insisted that the officer give her the dead man's social security number. Everything matched.

"I was in shock," Christine says of that awful moment.

When she got the news, she was wearing an oversized sweatshirt. The army's notification officer did not realize that she was pregnant. When she mentioned that she and Micheal were expecting their first child in October, he could only say, "Oh, God!"

On Father's Day, 2003, a pregnant Christine spent part of the day at the funeral home with Micheal. His body had been transported to Pennsylvania for burial, where there was a service with full military honors.

"I had pictures taken of Micheal's funeral. I know that sounds a bit morbid," Christine explains. "But since we have a baby who has never met [its] father, I thought it was important to document everything."

At Fort Carson, Colorado, there was a memorial service for the fallen sergeant. Hundreds of troops turned out to pay respect and tribute to Sergeant Dooley. At the conclusion of the service, one of the soldiers performed a roll call. He called out two names, and each of the soldiers answered, "Present." Then he called out Dooley's name.

In the chapel there was nothing but silence.

The soldier barked out his name again.

Still no answer.

"Sergeant Micheal E. Dooley!" he cried out for the third time.

There was only silence.

For his service, Micheal Dooley was posthumously honored with the Purple Heart and the Bronze Star.

On Tuesday, October 14, 2003, at 3:17 a.m., Christine delivered a healthy surprise bundle at Forbes Regional Hospital—a baby girl! She weighed nearly seven pounds and was nineteen-and-a-half inches long.

"I named her Shea Micheal Dooley, the name her daddy had chosen," Christine said.

In the delivery room with little Shea was a teddy bear her daddy had given her mother before he left for Iraq. Micheal had gone to the

Bear Factory, a store that lets customers make their own stuffed animals. The koala bear he created for Christine said, "I love you," when she pressed on his chest. His name was Lil' Soldier, and his job was to keep Christine company while Micheal was gone. The bear had another important duty too: Micheal wanted Lil' Soldier to go to the hospital with Christine if she had the baby before he could get home. For that reason, Micheal dressed the bear in scrubs.

"I slept with the bear every night, hugged him when I was sad, and took him to the hospital when I had Shea," Christine remembers. "Micheal had wanted me to give the bear to the baby after she was born, but I couldn't give it up right away. I waited until she was about two months old. Then I was ready to give it to her."

There was some local media interest in Baby Shea's birth. A few days after they got out of the hospital, Christine and her baby posed for the local news cameras. The baby was wearing a tee shirt that read, "My daddy, my hero." Surrounded by her family, the baby honored the father she would never know.

In the year after Micheal's death, Shea and her mother attended various memorial ceremonies. At one of them, Christine met Sergeant John Washburn for the first time. It was a special meeting for both of them.

While he was still in Iraq, Washburn told his wife, Michelle, all about Micheal and his death. Michelle had a bracelet made with Micheal's information on it and sent it to her husband overseas. John was wearing the bracelet the day he met Christine and Shea Dooley. He took it off his wrist and gave it to Micheal's baby girl.

On Father's Day, 2004, Christine took some time to visit a Web site honoring fallen heroes in Iraq. She posted the following message on the bulletin board:

Well, it's been slightly over a year now—it's hard to believe. I am proud of the way we got through it. I know his strength carried me when times I felt like I couldn't go any further. Now I have my own strength to live my life and deal with things as they are given to me. Today is Father's Day—it would have been his first one. I spent last year's Father's Day with him in the funeral home. I was alone with him, for his viewings didn't start till the next day. I put his favorite hat, watch, and his wedding band on him one last time. I also gave him seven roses. Six of them represented our cats and dogs, who he called his four-legged kids. And they truly were. The seventh one was from the unborn baby he gave me. He has given me a beautiful little girl to love. On days I felt like my heart had had too much, she was there to put more love into it. No matter where our lives take us, she will always be my miracle and strength. I have a wonderful family and wonderful friends who have gotten me through the past year. Without all the support I received, I don't know where I would be today. The first year is over, meaning I have done and gone through everything at least once. I feel like I have come out of a horrible storm. I am proud of myself and thankful for my support system. Micheal will always be in my heart and never forgotten. Happy Father's Day, Micheal. You should be proud of our little girl. She is awesome!

Baby Shea at her father's memorial

DOOLEY FAMILY COLLECTION

Love,

Christine

Before he left for Iraq, Micheal told Christine that his wife and his baby "completed his life." His last letter home shows just how much Sergeant Dooley was looking forward to being a dad.

Hey, baby,
May 23, 03
How are you and what are you doing? I am sitting here relaxing for a while. We just got word we are going further west in Iraq. We are going to secure a couple of towns near Syria. We will be on our own (my troop), about 180 km away from any supply lines. They said we will have to find most of our food and water. I think it will be cool! I know how to survive and will do it.

How is the baby doing? I hope he is doing fine. I know you are taking care of him and yourself. I have faith in you. I bet he is getting active now, kicking and moving around. I wish I was there to see all of this stuff I am missing. I want to feel him kick. When is your next ultrasound? Please send me a new picture of the baby when you get one. How are all my four-legged kids doing? I really miss them. I want some pictures of them too. And tell me everything they do or trouble they get into while I am gone.

I want pictures of you, to see how big your belly is getting. How much my baby is growing inside of you. Not being with you makes me weak. You are the link that makes my chain strong. You complete me in every way. I can't wait to come home and hold you in my arms! You were my first and last pen pal I will ever have. I think only one thing will change between us when I get home. We will not be as close as we used to be; we will be even closer. I mean that. I am going crazy without you.

I haven't really had time to write anyone except you, so could you let everyone know I am safe and have thought about them. Thank you.

Love, your husband,
Micheal

PS-Give all my four-legged kids a kiss and tell them Daddy loves them.

AFTERTHOUGHTS

Who are the soldiers that choose to serve our nation?

They have white faces.

They have black faces.

They have brown faces.

They are men.

They are women.

They are teenagers.

Some are in their 20's or 30's; others are in their 40's.

Some become soldiers; others are sailors. Some serve by performing mundane tasks, like cleaning, cooking, or driving a service vehicle. Others become hardened killing machines. They come from tiny rural communities, and huge urban sprawls.

But they all have one thing in common: duty. When their Commander-in-Chief sends them into battle, they bid their families farewell, and they go. These men and women, some of the best and brightest our nation has to offer, understand the risks they face. They serve in America's military not because it is easy, but because it must be done. The moment they take the oath, they devote their lives to the service of the United States.

"I, ____________________, "do solemnly swear that I will support and defend the Constitution of the United States against all enemies, foreign and domestic;

that I will bear true faith and allegiance to the same; and that I will obey the orders of the President of the United States and the orders of the officers appointed over me, according to regulations and the Uniform Code of Military Justice. So help me God."

No one wants war—not the president, not the American people, and especially not the members of the armed forces. We all want to live in peace, to enjoy the freedom that America gives us. But sometimes, we have no choice. The world changed on September 11, 2001. We became fully aware of the enemies that stand before us. It is against these enemies that the brave men and women in uniform now fight.

Over the next fifty or sixty years, Americans will sit down with their children and grandchildren to talk about that awful day in September and the war that followed it. They will remember the brave Americans who perished in the name of their country, so that we might all live with the blessings of American liberty.

Let them tell the soldiers' stories—how they served, and who they were. Let the letters and e-mails in this book remind us that all of the men and women who died fighting this war served with pride, and that, even under the harshest of conditions, their loved ones—parents, spouses, fiancées, and children—never left their minds.

Let us all remember their last words. And let those words ring true to future generations, so that those who sacrificed everything might never be forgotten.

APPENDIX
CONTACTING THE FAMILIES

The Pentagon will not release the addresses or telephone numbers of the families of fallen soldiers. Representatives will reply to any attempt at contact with this message: "We appreciate your concern, but we are unable to release mailing addresses of the military families due to the Privacy Act of 1974."

Each service branch will forward appropriate letters for you if you follow this procedure:

Write your letter, and place it in a stamped, unsealed envelope.

Write a cover letter to the casualty office explaining your purpose for writing.

Place your correspondence, the letter to the service person's family, and the unsealed, stamped envelope in a stamped, sealed envelope, and mail the entire package to the appropriate casualty office.

The casualty office will review your request, and then forward your letter to the family.

Army:
Director, Casualty/Memorial Affairs Operation Center
US Total Army Personnel Command
ATTN: TAPC-PED

2641 Eisenhower Avenue
Alexandria, VA 22331
Phone: 703-325-7960

Marine Corps:
Casualty Section
Code MHP-10
Washington, DC 20380-0001
Phone: 703-696-2061

Navy
Casualty Assistance Branch
NMPC-122
Washington, DC 20370-5120
Phone: 1-800-572-2126

Air Force:
500 C Street, West Suite 15
Randolph AFB, TX 78150-4717
Phone: 210-652-3727

I have established a Web site, which you can visit at *http://www.theirlastwords.com*. There you will find additional, up-to-date information about the memorial funds of the soldiers whose stories appear in this book.

I will also forward your messages and letters to the families of the fallen soldiers. Mail your correspondence to:

George G. Sheldon
Post Office Box 6238
Lancaster, PA 17607-6238